RESTLESS CONTINENT

RESTLESS CONTINENT

WEALTH, RIVALRY AND ASIA'S NEW GEOPOLITICS

MICHAEL WESLEY

OVERLOOK DUCKWORTH
NEW YORK • LONDON

First published in the United States and the United Kingdom in hardcover in 2016 by
Overlook Duckworth, Peter Mayer Publishers, Inc.

NEW YORK
141 Wooster Street
New York, NY 10012
www.overlookpress.com
For bulk and special sales please contact sales@overlookny.com,
or to write us at the above address.

LONDON
30 Calvin Street
London E1 6NW
www.ducknet.co.uk
For bulk and special sales please contact sales@duckworth-publishers.co.uk,
or write to us at the above address.

Cataloging-in-Publication Data is available from the Library of Congress

A catalogue record for this book is available from the British Library

Manufactured in the United States of America

ISBN: 978-1-4683-1298-0 (US)
ISBN: 978-0-7156-5087-5 (UK)

1 3 5 7 9 10 8 6 4 2

CONTENTS

Asia's Strategic Geography

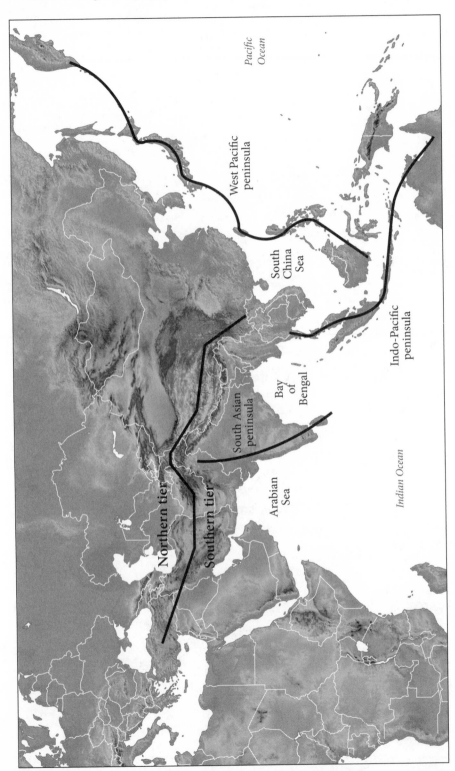

PREFACE

Only the passing of time will tell whether it was an act of decisive resolve or a gesture of impotence. As dawn broke over the waters of the South China Sea, at 6:40am on Tuesday, October 27, 2015, the USS *Lassen*, a guided missile destroyer, entered the waters within 12 nautical miles of the disputed Mischief and Subi Reefs. The sail-through had been long-planned and much anticipated. Some six months earlier, Secretary of Defense Ashton Carter had announced that the US Navy would assert its right to freedom of navigation close to those reefs, as part of a deepening dispute with China over the legal status of the South China Sea. Since the 1940s governments of China—both the Nationalist regime now exiled to Taiwan as well as the People's Republic—have claimed most of the South China Sea as sovereign territorial waters. Their claims have been disputed by other states bordering the Sea who assert their own, more limited territorial claims; as well as by the United States and some of its allies who claim the Sea is an international waterway according to international law. What gave such significance in 2015 to a relatively regular maritime patrol by a US warship was China's rapid conversion of eight low-lying reefs and rocks in the Spratley Islands group into artificial islands with dredged sand and concrete.

The plain-speaking head of US Pacific Command, Admiral Harry Harris, had proclaimed in early 2015 that by constructing more than four square kilometers of artificial landmass, Beijing had constructed a "great wall of sand" in the crucial international shipping thoroughfare. At stake was not just the constructions themselves, but what China could put on them. One artificial island had a runway large enough to accommodate the largest warplanes in the Chinese arsenal; others could conceivably host settlements, missiles, and troops.

The Chinese response to the *Lassen*'s sail-through was fast and shrill. Vice Foreign Minister Zhang Yesui summoned American Ambassador Max Baucus for an official dressing down over the United States' "extremely irresponsible" actions. An ensuing statement by the Chinese Foreign Ministry made sure there was little chance of misinterpretation: "The actions of the US warship have threatened China's sovereignty and security interests, jeopardized the safety of personnel and facilities on the reefs and damaged regional peace and stability." The next day, an editorial in the *Global Times*, one of the Chinese Communist Party's more nationalist mouthpieces, warned, "China…is not frightened to fight a war with the US in the region, and is determined to safeguard its national interests and dignity." As if to back up the *Global Times*' threat, two PLA Navy warships, the *Taizhou* and the *Lanzhou*, were dispatched to the vicinity of the Spratley Islands with orders to enforce China's sovereignty and deter any further "illegal activity." For its part, the United States was also quick to respond. In China on a pre-planned official visit, Admiral Harris spoke with customary clarity to a forum at Peking University: "We've been conducting freedom of navigation operations all over the world for decades…the South China Sea is not, and will not, be an exception."

As recent Sino-American confrontations go, the *Lassen* incident looks relatively minor. The risk of serious conflict between the two nuclear-armed powers appeared much more likely in March 1996, when a US aircraft carrier battle group sailed into the Taiwan Straits as a warning to Beijing to desist from aggressive missile tests and naval exercises intended to intimidate historic elections in Taiwan. Or again five years later when a Chinese fighter jet collided with a US EP-3 surveillance aircraft, resulting in a tense stand-off as Beijing refused to release the American plane and crew, which had emergency landed on Hainan Island. What makes the *Lassen* incident so much more significant are the stakes involved. How and when the United States asserts freedom of navigation and the manner in which China counters by asserting its claimed sovereign imperatives is about so much more than the status of a few partially-submerged rocks and reefs or even one of the world's most crucial shipping thoroughfares. It is, at base, a contest over primacy in Asia.

Primacy is a word in increasingly regular usage in recent years. This is significant because it is a word that lapses into disuse when it is assumed and uncontested, but it emerges from the shadows when it is under contention. Primacy is essentially the risk-management strategy of every great power in history. As history's great powers have risen and matured, their interests have expanded and evolved, and without exception, each has prioritized the ability to shape the behavior and tolerances of less powerful states to accommodate the great power's evolving interests. As Chapter 2 of this book points out, successive European powers contested for primacy in Asia: the Dutch supplanted the Portuguese, only to be toppled by the British. Cultural solidarity and geopolitical alignment don't matter in primacy contests, as the United States demonstrated as it slowly and methodically undermined British primacy in Asia during the early 20th century, and consciously built its own primacy on the foundations laid by Britain. Real primacy is effortless: the less coercion or co-option the great power needs to bend other states to its will, the greater and more complete is its primacy. Different great powers have used different means to achieve primacy: economic dynamism, ideologies, hierarchic relationships, shared interests, institutions and rules. Each great power in history has chosen the terms and means of its own primacy according to what international conditions will best allow it to preserve and extend its own power.

For most of the seven decades since the end of World War II, American primacy in Asia has rarely been discussed because it has been so complete. It has been a primacy based in liberal values, open trade and investment, freedom of access, and bilateral alliance structures. Even during the low points of America's postwar involvement in the region—the bitter stalemate of the Korean War or the retreat from Vietnam—the United States' ability to secure its preferences and shape the region to its own interests remained unchallenged and undiminished. It was the completeness of American primacy in Asia that allowed the region to develop at the fastest rates yet seen in human history, and to do so in an era of unprecedented peace and stability since the end of the Vietnam War.

Ironically, America's achievement has brought about the conditions for the most serious challenge to its primacy in Asia in 70 years. China's explosive growth, which has seen its economy grow to the world's second largest in just three decades, has awakened the prerogatives and interests of a rival great power. As it has grown richer and stronger, China has come to see the conditions of American primacy as a great risk to itself. From Beijing's perspective, it is American primacy that renders it unable to achieve China's historical unity by absorbing Taiwan, which it has always seen as a renegade province. American primacy emboldens the Japanese to refuse to atone adequately in Beijing's eyes for its conduct during World War II, just as it emboldens some of the Southeast Asian countries bordering the South China Sea to contest Beijing's assertion that its waters are China's sovereign territory. American primacy underpins Beijing's constant anxiety that Washington will mobilize a containment coalition to constrain and choke off China's growth—or at the very least threaten the flow of energy China so desperately needs as it sails through the Indian Ocean and Southeast Asia's chokepoints. In simple terms, living under American primacy constitutes unacceptable risk; Beijing's only option is to try to replace American primacy in Asia with Chinese primacy.

China challenges American primacy in Asia on two levels. One is a direct challenge to the United States' ability to access and operate in the waters of the western Pacific with safety. Beijing's military build-up has seen it invest heavily in the weapons systems that can raise the level of risk for the US Navy to operate along Asia's eastern coastlines. The second level is an indirect challenge to the credibility of the United States to be able to guarantee the stability and peace of the region and support the interests of its allies and partners. As Beijing prosecutes territorial disputes with Japan in the East China Sea and the Philippines and Vietnam in the South China Sea, it is really probing American resolve to stand behind its allies and partners in their defense of their interests. Beijing also knows that Washington's need to prove its credibility has a dark side: that it could risk being dragged into a conflict by a smaller ally willing to play on America's anxieties about its own credibility.

The Obama administration has been well aware of the Chinese challenge and the stakes involved for the United States. Writing in the journal *Foreign Policy* in October 2011, Secretary of State Hillary Clinton observed: "One of the most important tasks of American statecraft over the next decade will…be to lock in a substantially increased investment—diplomatic, economic, strategic, and otherwise—in the Asia Pacific region." For Clinton, the contest in Asia had global implications: "A strategic turn to the [Asian] region fits logically into our overall global effort to secure and sustain America's global leadership"; it was a strategic choice she compared to the Marshall Plan and founding of NATO sixty years earlier: "just as our post-World War II commitment to building a comprehensive and lasting transatlantic network of institutions and relationships… the time has come for the United States to make similar investments as a Pacific power."[1] One month later, in a speech to a joint sitting of the Australian Parliament, President Obama proclaimed, "the United States is turning our attention to the vast potential of the Asia Pacific region…the United States will play a larger and long-term role in shaping this region and its future." By mid-2012, the administration's resolve had been written into strategic policy: the United States would "rebalance" its attention away from the Middle East towards the Asia Pacific region, where 60 percent of its naval, space, and cyber assets would be positioned.[2]

The American "rebalance" to Asia seems to have had little effect on the challenge to the United States' primacy in the region. Beijing has, if anything, intensified its own primacy bid despite the Obama administration's resolve. Within two years of the policy's announcement, China had proclaimed an air defense identification zone around disputed territories with Japan and South Korea in the East China Sea, and begun daily military incursions into Japanese territorial waters and airspace. It prevailed in a tense confrontation with the Philippines over the Scarborough Shoal in the South China Sea, and positioned an oil exploration platform in Vietnam's territorial waters, provoking rioting in several Vietnamese cities. India voiced concerns over repeated and escalating Chinese incursions across their disputed border high in the eastern Himalayas. And while American allies such as Japan, the Philippines, and Australia have tightened their relationships with Washington, and the United States has acquired new security "partners" such as Singapore, New Zealand, and—more startlingly—Vietnam and India, it is very apparent that such countries are no longer content to rely on American power alone to ensure their security. Across

Asia, arms acquisitions and military expansions have been beating a rising tempo. Meanwhile Beijing seems to have the strategic initiative, able to choose the time, place, and nature of its assertion of primacy, increasingly confident that no other country—including the United States—is willing to jeopardize its economic relationship with China in order to resist China's encroachments on the familiar regional order.

This is the context through which the *Lassen*'s sail-through needs to be viewed. The freedom of navigation rights that Secretary Carter and Admiral Harris asserted are more than legal technicalities in an international waterway: they are both symbolic of and central to the liberal trading order that has both underpinned and been upheld by American primacy in Asia for 70 years. The question for the United States and its allies in Asia is whether the *Lassen* and subsequent US warships that chart similar courses will convince Beijing to moderate its bid for primacy in relation to the South China Sea. For China the question is whether its gradual alteration of the facts on the ground—the artificial islands, the airstrips and docks, potentially settlers, soldiers, and weapons—will allow it to slowly assert primacy over the South China Sea without risking destabilizing conflict with America and its allies and partners.

A look at America's history in Asia suggests that the outcome of the current struggle for primacy will depend as much on Asia's own internal dynamics as it will on what the United States chooses to do. Since the American Revolution, Asia has been the font and proving ground of American wealth and power. In the post-Revolutionary decades, the access of American traders to the wealth of the orient, unimpeded by colonial rivalries or the monopoly provisions of imperial trading conglomerates, provided the young Republic with the necessary early surge of capital to finance its fledgling banks and infrastructure.[3] It was the promise of Asian markets for the surging American economy in the late 19th century that eventually drew the United States into the imperial competition across the Pacific: Guam, Hawai'i, Samoa, the Philippines. Asia was the great exception to American isolationism: Even as the United States stood aloof from the power politics in Europe, the Middle East, and Africa, it remained vigorously involved in the diplomacy of Asia through the 19th and early 20th centuries. As it rose to world power, the United States expended almost 60 percent of its war dead in Asian conflicts. When it confronted the threat of communism following World War II, it was the loss of China to communism—not Poland, Hungary, or Czechoslovakia—that provoked a national crisis within the United States. It was a great power deal in Asia, between President Nixon and Chairman Mao, that ultimately enabled the United States to prevail in the Cold War.

Restless Continent examines these local power dynamics within Asia. It looks at the effects of Asia's rapid enrichment and empowerment on that continent's international relations. How the various forces described in these pages play out—economic interdependence, military competition, cultural rivalries, contests of values, alignments and enmities—will have major implications for America's role in this region which has always been so vital for the United States' broader global role. How Asia's new geopolitics play out, what mixture of coercion, co-option, and geoeconomic statecraft, will determine what options are open to the United States. And ultimately, the combination of local power dynamics and US responses will have great consequences for the rest of the world in the 21st century.

At this stage, there are three possible futures for America in Asia, each recalling a particular period of United States involvement in the region. On the one hand, the rebalance and continued American resolve could face down the Chinese challenge to its primacy and return the future to a pattern that characterized the most recent past—continuing uncontested US primacy. For this to occur, the dynamics described in the pages ahead would need to play out in a particular way. The forces of rivalry and contestation would need to be demonstrably costly in terms of economic growth and dynamism in the region. Asia's countries would need to come to a realization, individually and collectively, that their continued economic dynamism and interdependence were more important than the contests over territory and deference that animate much of the region's international relations. There would need to be a collective agreement, including by Beijing, that American primacy is the lowest-cost and most durable underpinning of continuing prosperity for Asia.

Another possibility is that the United States will enter a period of bipolar competition with a rising Asian power, as occurred in the early twentieth century. While the other significant countries in Asia and the Pacific are interested parties, they would individually and collectively need to conclude that they have little impact on the escalating Sino-American competition. Again, such an outcome relies on the cards in the current geopolitical mix in Asia to fall in certain ways. The contest between China and the United States would play out in intensifying geoeconomic competition—trading blocs, embargoes, manipulation of resource and financial flows—while they also competed militarily. The other countries of the region would react by trying as best they can to protect their interests from collateral damage. Perhaps the zero-sum nature of the competition would eventually lead the countries of Asia to choose sides, as economic and security blocs develop. In such a scenario, America only remains in part of Asia—and perhaps not necessarily that part of Asia that is most economically or strategically vital to it.

A third possibility is that Asia will see the rise of not one but several great powers. The rise of China has touched off competitive and defensive reactions from several countries around it, which for cultural and material reasons are apprehensive about the prospect of living under Chinese primacy. While not yet competing with China, several of these countries have the heft and geographic position to seriously complicate China's bid for primacy. Japan and India leap to mind; one must also think carefully about Russia, Indonesia, and maybe Iran. Already there is a fluidity to shifting alignments in Asia that portends a genuinely multipolar system in which patterns of alignment and enmity overlap. When it last confronted a multipolar order in Asia, in the 19th century when several European powers and Japan competed for access to the riches of the orient, the United States participated in the competition while increasingly seeking to set boundaries on the contest by asserting the Open Door principles and opposing exclusive spheres of influence. As a detached but principled participant, the United States acted as an important stabilizer of what could have been destructive competition. Such a future would see the United States as both a participant in a shifting multipolar order, and a power that seeks to impose limits and standards on that multipolar order.

This is why the international relations of Asia are so important to the United States and ultimately the world. We are used to hearing pundits proclaiming the shift of the world's economic and strategic center of gravity to Asia, but few have explored what exactly this means. A continent with 60 percent of the world's population, more than half the world's production and consumption capacity, and an increasingly potent collection of military arsenals is one that deserves much more attention than it currently receives. If this continent emerges peaceful, stable, and prosperous, it bodes well for global affairs in our century. But if the patterns of rivalry and mistrust deepen, we're in for a much more uncertain future. There is therefore no more important challenge to policymakers, academics, and the public than understanding the drivers of Asia's new geopolitics. These are the subjects of *Restless Continent*.

INTRODUCTION

At 10 am on 30 January 2013, in the cold gunmetal-grey waters of the East China Sea, a Chinese Jiangwei-II frigate locked its fire-control radar onto the *Yudachi*, the largest destroyer in the potent Japanese navy, 3 kilometres away. Fire-control radar calculates the range, velocity and size of an enemy target and is the prelude to firing a lethal missile.[1] The *Yudachi* immediately took evasive action. The confrontation resulted in little more than angry denunciations from Tokyo and Beijing, but it could have had much more dramatic consequences. The *Yudachi* could have activated its fire-control radar and perhaps even fired at the Chinese frigate in self-defence. With no crisis-management mechanism in place between Asia's two most powerful countries, and with uncompromising territorial claims and nationalism at fever pitch at home, the chances of such an incident escalating into a major conflict are relatively high. Given that the United States is an ally of Japan, the possibility that it could have developed into a nuclear standoff was uncomfortably real.[2]

Just over a century before this incident, in waters 1500 kilometres to the north, a naval exchange of fire began a war that was to plunge East Asia into almost continuous conflict for the next half century, claiming millions of lives and sowing the seeds of the region's current tensions. On 25 July 1894, three Japanese cruisers attacked two Chinese warships and a troop transport near Feng Island on the Korean coast. In the war that followed, the chaotic forces of the tottering Qing empire were quickly dispatched by the industrial efficiency of Japan's army and navy. Korea, the Ryukyu Islands and Taiwan, for centuries under Chinese suzerainty, would become the first territories of the Japanese Empire. The shock of Japan's defeat of China reverberated across the world. Following the stunning Japanese victory in the battle of Yalu River, the Parisian *Le Journal des Débats Politiques et Littéraires* proclaimed, 'The Battle of the Yalu is an important date in history . . . if Goethe had participated in the Battle of the Yalu, it is probable he would have said as he did to his compatriots at Valmy, "Here and today begins a new historical era and you can say that you have witnessed it".[3]

The shock of the first Sino-Japanese war was so much greater because it was so unexpected. East Asia had experienced almost three centuries of tranquility and prosperity after the signing of a peace treaty between Korea and Japan in 1609. Thereafter, China, Japan, Korea and the Ryukyu Kingdom managed their diplomatic and trade relations carefully and in accordance with shared Confucian precepts of order and obligation. Each society existed as an independent kingdom, while acknowledging its debt to the fount of learning and cultural refinement of China. Trade and tribute flowed in a regular and regulated way between the four kingdoms, even as all four moved, from the early seventeenth century, to shut out disturbing influences from further afield.

By the mid-nineteenth century, however, this insular subregion of East Asia was under assault. Instead of the nomadic raiders of old, Imperial China faced the ruthless efficiency of an industrialising Russian empire that was seizing territory on its inner borders. Nibbling at China's southern coasts were avaricious and arrogant

Europeans: the British, French, Dutch, Portuguese and Germans. The Dutch and the Portuguese had been greedily eyeing Japan as well. The most insistent, for the Japanese and Koreans at least, were a sanctimonious and acquisitive people from the other side of the Pacific Ocean – the Americans. Acute observers in Japan, Korea and China soon realised that the great demand for what they produced – silver, silks, porcelain, metalware – would make assaults on their seclusion unceasing; their seclusion and lack of interest in western goods in turn made them vulnerable.

While elites in China and Korea regarded the west with haughty contempt, the forces of reform quickly gained the upper hand in Japan, overthrowing the centuries-old regime of the shoguns. The rapidity with which the Meiji reformers replaced Japan's feudal order with the institutions and industries of modern European societies has few parallels in history. Japan adopted western models of mass society and urbanisation, universal education, industrial development, democracy and constitutional monarchy, and military organisation and training. What distinguished these reforms was not just their rapidity but also their comprehensiveness. While China's and Korea's reformers had been able to bring about minor improvements – a modern shipyard here or a state-of-the-art railway line there – their societies remained stubbornly resistant to renovation or change. The result was stagnation and decline in Korea and China, while Japan's economy and population expanded astonishingly quickly. In the quarter century between the Meiji Restoration and the outbreak of the first Sino-Japanese War, the Japanese economy grew by 65 per cent; it would take just another fifteen years for it to double in size.[4] During the last quarter of the nineteenth century, Japan's rate of economic growth, at an average of 7 per cent per annum, was matched only by that of the United States. The industrial share of the Japanese economy would grow from one-fifth in 1887 to over one-half in 1940.[5]

The most important effect of the sudden divergence in the economic fortunes of Japan and its neighbours was on mutual perceptions. Watching the Europeans' cavalier humiliation of China, and the hidebound Qing Dynasty's inability to respond effectively, Japanese admiration for Chinese culture and learning curdled into contempt. A mid-seventh-century slogan 'Japanese spirit and Chinese learning' was revived and changed to 'Japanese spirit and Western learning'.[6] Almost overnight, all vestiges of Confucian learning were ridiculed and rejected, and replaced by the most advanced western techniques and doctrines. Chinese elites were horrified; having long thought of the Japanese as their younger brothers, they saw this as the ultimate rejection of the core Confucian principle of filial piety. The relationship soon degenerated to an exchange of insults, with official Chinese letters referring to the Japanese as *woren* (dwarf pirates). The attitudes and capabilities of the industrial age played out on a terrain etched with old cultural rivalries and stereotypes. The Qing court saw its duty as pulling the wayward Japanese into line, while Japan felt it needed to decisively demonstrate its superiority over China or else it would continue to be treated as an abject and backward Asian nation.

Yet for all the shock of its eruption in July 1894, there was something oddly familiar about the first Sino-Japanese War: the terrain on which it was fought. Chinese and Japanese forces had fought over the Korean Peninsula before. In the late thirteenth century, in the waters of the East China Sea, the Japanese desperately fought off two successive invasion attempts launched from the Korean Peninsula by the forces of China's Mongol Yuan Dynasty. Then, in the late sixteenth century, Chinese and Korean forces combined to fight a Japanese invasion force led by the shogun Toyotomi Hideyoshi. Media commentary in Japan and China made frequent reference to heroes and villains of previous wars. Little wonder that a member of the Japanese Diet mused after the end of the first Sino-Japanese War, 'What the Balkan Peninsula has so long been to Europe, the peninsula of Korea has for centuries been to the Far East – a "haunted place" wherein lurked the unceasing source of danger to the peace of the Orient'.[7] How right he was. Within a decade, Japan and Russia would fight a full-scale conflict in the East China Sea and China's Liaotung Peninsula, and then, having formally annexed Korea in 1910, Japanese forces would push deep into Manchuria and China itself. Even after the Japanese were defeated and expelled in 1945, the Korean Peninsula would be plunged into a brutal war from 1950 to 1953.

Hindsight is seductive. It is tempting to conclude that statesmen and strategists should have realised that the outbreak of hostilities off Feng Island in July 1894 was likely to blaze into a region-wide war within decades. Surely contemporary observers could see that the three centuries of peace in East Asia had crumbled? That the rapid change in the relative strengths of Japan, China and Korea – and, more importantly, the effects on long-held self-perceptions and cultural rivalries – contained the seeds of decades of incessant warfare and brutality? That the geography of the Korean Peninsula would once more become the epicentre of a bloody struggle?

Of course such expectations are unreasonable. Underlying trends and conditions are necessary but not sufficient conditions of history. There is so much serendipity, so many decisions and confluences, that the best we can do as we look into the future is to identify the emerging trends and structural conditions that the serendipitous events are inspired by. Are the *Yudachi* incident of 2013 and other recent dangerous confrontations in the East and South China seas marginal distractions at the dawn of another age of stability and prosperity, or are they the harbingers of an era of rivalry and conflict?

What sort of future awaits the world's largest continent as it enters an age of global wealth and power? Has Asia's recent past, an era of remarkable peace and prosperity, set the pattern for the continent's future? Will the stable economic miracle years between the end of the Vietnam War and now be seen as a temporary golden age? This last question animates the first chapter of *Restless Continent: Wealth, Rivalry and Asia's New Geopolitics.* Specifically, it asks what brought about four decades of peace and stability after the fall of Saigon and how likely these conditions are to endure.

In this book, I argue that the future of this restless continent will be shaped by two trends and two conditions. Chapter 2 investigates the first trend, the deepening interdependence of Asia's economies; in particular, the deepening mutual dependence related to manufacturing and services, as well as flows of energy, which are beginning to unite Asia's subregions in ways that are likely to have far-ranging economic and strategic effects.

Economic interdependence is the good news story of the recent past – it allowed Western Europe to transform itself from a realm of constant conflict to one of peace and prosperity. But Chapter 3 raises important questions about whether Asia's interdependence will bring similar results. As their economies grow, Asian states rely on the global economy for markets, resources, energy and investment. But the scale and pace of their rise means that Asia's larger states are often afflicted by 'strategic claustrophobia' – a fear that, either by accident or by design, they will be denied the markets, resources, energy and investment they need to continue their brittle internal evolution. It is inevitable that Asian states, for so long compliant with regional and global rules and rules designed by others, will increasingly insist that these change to be more conducive to their continued economic development and security.

Chapter 4 examines the reawakening sensitivity to civilisational hierarchies. A sense of cultural pride, often harkening back to pre-colonial golden ages, has been a powerful rallying symbol for many new states in Asia as they grapple with overcoming their colonial past and forging unity from ethnic and religious diversity. These recovered histories have imbued Asia's international relations with prickly rivalry. Assertions of civilisational pride, and even hints of condescension, are met with vigorous resistance and loud counter-claims. Territorial disagreements, war histories and differential rates of economic growth quickly acquire undertones of uncompromising nationalism. Alongside the growing interdependence and assertiveness of Asia's rising powers is the constant tension of deep cultural rivalries that erode trust and compromise.

The fifth chapter considers the geographic stage on which Asia's rivalries will play out. It argues that, even during long periods of peace, the rules and understandings of international affairs are underpinned by a subterranean structure of force that determines which rules can be ignored or challenged and which will be enforced. The growing wealth and assertiveness of Asia's states creates a power paradox: the more powerful countries become, the more vulnerable they feel. Fears of encirclement are driving an escalating arms race across the continent, leading to a shift in the latent structure of force that underpins the continent's rules and institutions; a shift that is playing out across two different geographic settings. One is predominantly littoral and maritime. Asia's crowded and booming Indian and Pacific Ocean coasts and waterways have become a source of nagging anxiety as well strategic opportunity for the continent's jostling powers, and the collective result is an ever-more contested and crowded maritime domain, particularly around Asia's distinctive bays and peninsulas. The other setting is terrestrial. On the vast steppes of north and central Asia, two continental empires face each other warily across a landlocked archipelago of small, isolated and internally unstable states. Although this realm appears more peaceful than the maritime realm, it could spin into strategic rivalry every bit as intense and complicated.

Chapter 6 draws together these trends and structural conditions. A new era of international affairs has already dawned in Asia in which the two opposed dynamics of rivalry and interdependence constrain each other. The collective interest of Asian states in peace and development will likely make for a rough but shifting equilibrium, one that relies increasingly on innovations in statecraft and institutions for its continuance. Asia's international relations will more and more shape those of the world, but as the ambit of Asia's influence widens this will also create opportunities for other states and institutions to shape in turn the compromises and understandings of a restless continent.

1

PEACE DIVIDENDS

Dawn broke clear and still over Saigon on the last day of April 1975. A helicopter settled carefully onto the rooftop of the American embassy, whipping up the tear gas in harried tendrils, making the marines cough and their eyes stream. They were the last of the 200 Americans who had retreated upwards from the ground floor, locking doors behind them with steel bars, dumping furniture and tear-gas grenades into the stairways and lift wells. Below them, hundreds of Vietnamese, many of them employees at the embassy, were pleading to be evacuated, some lifting their children and imploring the Americans to take them. But their fate had been decided by messages carried in on two helicopters. One, handwritten, from CINCPAC – the commander-in-chief of American forces in the Pacific – arrived at 3.15 am: 'On the basis of the reported total of 726 refugees, CINCPAC is authorized to send 19 helicopters and no more' – the last two words underlined twice. Then, at 4.42 am came a presidential order: only Americans are to be evacuated.[1]

The mortar blasts were crumping closer as the last marine, Juan Valdez, clambered into the belly of the helicopter. It lifted off at 7.53 am and flew towards the rising sun, flanked by two Cobra combat helicopters. As the convoy flew over the coastline, the marines cheered and took pictures. Awaiting their arrival on the USS *Blue Ridge*, the last American ambassador to the Republic of Vietnam, Graham Martin, read three congratulatory cables – from President Gerald Ford, Secretary of State Henry Kissinger and National Security Adviser Brent Scowcroft.

Operation Frequent Wind – the evacuation of the last Americans and Vietnamese refugees from South Vietnam between 28 and 30 April 1975 – was a remarkable achievement – a modern-day Dunkirk. Marine pilots had flown for an average of thirteen hours a day, and some for eighteen hours straight. The evacuation helicopters flew 689 sorties, 160 of them at night. They evacuated 2,206 people, including 1,373 Americans, from the United States embassy. The eight ships of the evacuation fleet took aboard a total of 29,783 refugees.

That there were no losses or crashes was in large part due to the decision by the North Vietnamese Army and the Provisional Revolutionary Government (PRG) in South Vietnam to let the evacuees leave unmolested, while pressing ahead with their occupation of Saigon. As the last helicopter lifted off the embassy roof, North Vietnamese tanks and troops sped through streets festooned with PRG banners and white flags, and strewn with discarded fatigues, boots, helmets and cartridge belts of the soldiers of the Army of the Republic of Vietnam. At 12.15 pm, Tank 879 of the 203rd Brigade, driven by Bui Duc Mai, roared down Thong Nhut Boulevard, momentarily overshooting the entrance to the American embassy. It made a three-point turn and smashed through the heavy iron gates. Squadron commander Bui Quang Than scaled the facade to tear down the Republic of Vietnam flag and replace it with that of the PRG.

Thirteen days earlier, a thousand miles to the west, the communist forces of the Khmer Rouge had taken the capital of Cambodia, Phnom Penh. In three months' time, the communist Pathet Lao would take Vientiane, to complete their triumph in Laos. Communist rule had come to Indochina, despite the deaths of 58,209 Americans that resulted from trying to prevent it. The most powerful country in human history had been beaten for the first time. The Harvard sociologist Daniel Bell proclaimed the end of American exceptionalism in the journal *The Public Interest*: 'There is no longer Manifest Destiny or Mission [for America]. We have not been immune from the corruption of power. We have not been the exception ... our mortality now lies before us.'[2]

The Triumph of Pragmatism

Retreat from Saigon brought to an end the era of universalism in American foreign policy: the belief that the United States had to act to turn back communism whenever and wherever it threatened to escape its boundaries in the heart of Eurasia; the belief that a victory for communism anywhere was a mortal blow to the free world; the belief that America had such vast power it could – and should – lead the defence of freedom everywhere. As the embodiment of a young, confident America, President John F. Kennedy had pledged in his inaugural address that the United States would 'pay any price, bear any burden, meet any hardship, support any friend, oppose any foe, in order to assure the survival and the success of liberty'. It was the man Kennedy beat narrowly in the presidential race of 1960, the man who would ultimately prevail in the race for the presidency eight years later, who would quietly dismantle American universalism in Asia.

The Richard Nixon who entered the White House in January 1969 was a different man from the ranting anti-communist who had been plucked from obscurity to be Dwight D. Eisenhower's vice-president in 1952. He had spent the years following his defeat in the 1960 presidential race thinking hard about how the world worked:

travelling, reading widely, questioning the leaders and diplomats he met closely. In Henry Kissinger, his pudgy, owlish national security adviser, he found a kindred mind. Nixon and Kissinger believed that, since the end of the Second World War, power, the very currency of international affairs, had changed: diffusing out of the hands of the superpowers towards smaller countries and even stateless movements, as well as fracturing into various forms – military, political, economic – that worked differently and even could contradict each other.[3] Consequently, the overriding goal Nixon had so fervently believed in as Eisenhower's vice-president – the containment and rollback of communism – had been displaced in Nixon's mind by a new foreign policy talisman: stability. No longer was it an all-or-nothing fight against communism; given the diffused and fractured nature of power, a setback in one region could be compensated for by gains elsewhere. Stability and détente between the nuclear-armed superpowers could be built by seeking stability in each of the world's regions and subregions.[4]

For all of their new thinking, Nixon and Kissinger faced a very real world problem: the United States was stuck in the agonising trap of the Vietnam War. While they had jettisoned the belief that a setback in Vietnam would be a mortal blow to the free world, they had replaced it with a different neurosis: that a humiliating withdrawal would corrode America's reputation among its allies and embolden world communism. And yet, every month the marines fought on in Vietnam deepened the immobility of American diplomacy elsewhere, isolating it from its closest allies, stripping it of moral capital and giving leverage to its competitors. At home the war was tearing American society apart. Knowing this, the North Vietnamese Politburo remained stubbornly reluctant to entertain any overtures for peace talks.

Nixon's solution to the war in Vietnam, and his formula for American foreign policy after the end of universalism, emerged in the unlikely setting of a balmy evening in the 'Top o' the Mar' officers' mess in the American base on Guam. Nixon and his entourage had stopped at Guam on the way to his first presidential visit to Asia, in part to coincide with the splashdown of the first Apollo moon mission. Speaking off the record to the travelling media pack, Nixon observed:

> As we look at Asia, it poses, in my view, over the long haul, looking down to the end of the century, the greatest threat to the peace of the world, and, for that reason the United States should continue to play a significant role. It also poses, it seems to me, the greatest hope for progress in the world – progress in the world because of the ability, the resources, the ability of the people, the resources physically that are available in this part of the world. And for these reasons, I think we need policies that will see that we play a part and a part that is appropriate to the conditions that we will find.[5]

That part, the president continued, would see America, while maintaining its treaty commitments, playing a supporting rather than a leading role: 'as far as the problems of internal security are concerned, as far as the problems of military defense, except for the threat of a major power involving nuclear weapons, that the United States is going to encourage and has a right to expect that this problem will be increasingly handled by, and the responsibility for it taken by, the Asian nations themselves'. This doctrine, which came to bear Nixon's name, was to be emphatically restated in a presidential message the following February: 'America cannot – and will not – conceive all the plans, design all the programs, execute all the decisions and undertake all the defense of the free world. We will help where it makes a real difference and is considered in our interest'.[6]

The Nixon Doctrine saw American troop numbers reduced in Vietnam, while a policy of 'Vietnamisation', channelling American military and development aid to Saigon, enabled South Vietnam to amass the fourth-largest armed forces on earth. But still Nixon and Kissinger could find no way to end America's intervention without what they believed would be a crippling loss of credibility. Hanoi remained unprepared to compromise, while Nixon worried that if he escalated the war to force the North Vietnamese to the negotiating table, it could provoke Chinese intervention, and he'd have another version of the Korean War on his hands. The solution to his predicament lay in the unlikeliest of places.

As Zhou Enlai stood on the tarmac of Beijing airport on a cold grey morning on 21 February 1972, it was arguably one of the most dangerous moments of his perilous life. That Zhou, the premier of China, had survived thus far the ravages of Mao Zedong's Cultural Revolution against 'bourgeois elements' in Chinese society and purges of other senior leaders was nothing short of extraordinary. Zhou had worked quietly behind the scenes to curb the worst excesses of the Cultural Revolution, including persuading Mao not to raze the Forbidden City. Dag Hammarskjold, the urbane Swedish United Nations Secretary-General, had remarked on meeting Zhou that for the first time in his life he had felt uncivilised in the presence of a civilised man – not exactly a trait that was valued by the marauding gangs of Red Guards during the Cultural Revolution. Now Zhou was awaiting the arrival of Air Force One, carrying President Nixon, a man who had once fulminated against the 'loss of China' to the communists. It was during Nixon's vice-presidency that the American secretary of state, John Foster Dulles, had refused to shake Zhou's proffered hand at an earlier peace conference on Vietnam in Geneva.

Zhou Enlai was a pragmatist. He was welcoming Nixon not because he wanted to dismantle the Chinese communist revolution but because he wanted to save it.[7] Rarely had China been so isolated and threatened as in the early 1970s. It had been shut out of the United Nations. Japan and most of Southeast Asia refused to recognise it diplomatically. Its developing influence in Indonesia had ended in the blood-drenched overthrow of the Beijing-friendly President Sukarno and the massacre of tens of thousands of Indonesian Communist Party members and ethnic Chinese. India, its non-aligned partner of the 1950s, watched it with bruised hostility across the Himalayan mountain passes after a sharp border war in 1962. The enduring hostility of the United States and deep isolation abroad were complemented internally by the fanatical orgy of the Cultural Revolution, which had suffocated economic growth, persecuted hundreds of millions and killed between one and three million people.

Most alarmingly, communist China's one significant alliance, with the Soviet Union, had broken down into deep antagonism amid mutual accusations of ideological betrayal, nuclear bad faith and conflicting territorial claims. Red Guards had attacked the Soviet embassy, placing it under virtual siege in 1967 and renaming the road outside 'Anti-Revisionism Street'. In 1968, Zhou told a visiting Albanian delegation that there had been over 2000 violations of the Chinese border territories by the Soviet Union. Moscow had begun a massive troop build-up: from seventeen divisions the Red Army would grow to fifty-four divisions along their mutual border. When a clash occurred in March 1969 on a disputed island in the Ussuri River called Zhenbao by the Chinese and Damansky by the Russians, the Soviet side responded with its biggest artillery barrage since the Second World War. Beijing had watched Soviet tanks stream into Prague in 1968 in the name of 'socialist orthodoxy', and wondered whether the focus of the Brezhnev Doctrine would soon turn to the east.[8]

To the south, Beijing worried that the war in Vietnam would draw it into yet another catastrophic conflict with the United States. Beijing feared another Korean War as much as Washington did.

Chinese leaders also fretted that the United States would retaliate against China's support of North Vietnam by backing efforts by Chinese nationalist forces on Taiwan to overthrow the Communist Party on the mainland. Zhou had been gently pressing Hanoi to rely less on Chinese assistance and to begin to compromise with the Americans; the North Vietnamese had reacted angrily, pointedly praising Moscow's 'selfless' intervention in Czechoslovakia in defence of socialist orthodoxy and solidarity. As Hanoi gravitated towards Moscow and India signed the Treaty of Peace, Friendship and Cooperation with the Soviet Union, Beijing's sense of isolation deepened.[9]

As President Nixon left the steps of Air Force One and, in front of a People's Liberation Army honour guard and a small crowd of onlookers, firmly shook Zhou Enlai's hand, the elements of a tacit agreement between the United States and China were already in place. Henry Kissinger had made a series of visits to China, beginning with a dramatic secret visit in July 1971. Zhou and Kissinger had agreed on some groundbreaking compromises: China and the United States needed to cooperate to contain an increasingly aggressive Soviet Union; Washington would not support any attempt from Taiwan to overthrow the government of the mainland; Beijing would tacitly accept the need for an American tactical escalation of the Vietnam War as a way of bringing about a strategic retreat. As Moscow tried to isolate it in Asia and the Communist bloc, China needed to end its isolation; Chairman Mao had told Kissinger, 'we should draw a horizontal line [through] the United States, Japan, China, Pakistan, Turkey and Europe' against the Soviet Union's intrigues.[10]

Nixon's visit to China culminated in the issue of one of the most remarkable documents in diplomatic history. The 'Shanghai Communiqué', signed on 28 February 1972, presented to the world a clear statement of the great differences between the United States and China, as each side included separate passages setting out its position on regional security issues, from Vietnam to the Korean Peninsula, Taiwan and the subcontinent. Zhou had insisted the communiqué not try to massage away the substantial divergences between Beijing and Washington, in large part to assuage domestic critics on both sides as well as to reassure allies. But despite the differences, the communiqué established three key points of agreement: the need to normalise Sino-American relations, the need to reduce the threat of military conflict, and Beijing's and Washington's shared opposition to any attempt at 'hegemony' in Asia.

It was not until 16 December 1978 that China and the United States reached final agreement on the establishment of diplomatic relations. When Nixon's successor Gerald Ford visited Beijing in late 1975 to push normalisation negotiations along, Zhou was in hospital battling terminal cancer and Deng Xiaoping had taken over as Ford's negotiating partner. Deng had just been rehabilitated after being purged during the Cultural Revolution and was aware that he was being watched with suspicion by the extremist 'Gang of Four' who had taken power from an ailing Mao Zedong. Despite his hardline negotiating style, Deng believed in the inevitability of Sino-American rapprochement. He urged the Americans not to be too impatient and force a suboptimal compromise. 'It should always be possible to find a way to solve problems,' he told George Bush, the head of the American Liaison Office in China in November 1974, 'we may wait if the conditions are not right.' Deng was convinced that normalisation of China's relations with the United States was necessary to the reform and opening up of the Chinese economy.[11]

The long period of negotiation between Kissinger's secret visit and the establishment of diplomatic relations on 1 January 1979 allowed a remarkable meeting of minds between China and the United States. Because they had no diplomatic relationship, Beijing and Washington couldn't use formal treaties to build trust and comity; rather they relied on a series of personal dialogues and relationships between Chinese leaders and their American counterparts, both Republican and Democrat. As they talked, American and Chinese statesmen built the foundations of pragmatic peace in Asia. American withdrawal from Vietnam was twinned with a firm commitment to its alliances and security commitments in the Pacific: with Japan, the Republic of Korea, Taiwan, the Philippines, Thailand, Australia and New Zealand. Washington had, in effect, abandoned an intent to project power onto the Asian continent, while remaining committed to holding the ring against aggression or infiltration in the islands and peninsulas of the western Pacific.

Meanwhile, the mutual non-aggression pact between China and the United States contributed to Beijing's growing sense that its energies should be directed towards change within rather than beyond its borders. After 1949, commitment to world revolution had led China to sponsor communist insurgencies throughout Asia, confirming and deepening the hostility and loathing of its neighbours towards Beijing. Even China's relations with fellow communist regimes were fractious. When Vietnam, angered by the expulsions of ethnic Vietnamese and border provocations by the Khmer Rouge, launched a full-scale invasion of Cambodia in December 1978, Beijing's support for Hanoi turned to hostility. Furious at Hanoi's invasion of Cambodia, its ingratitude for Beijing's support in fighting off the Americans, its alignment with Moscow and its persecution of ethnic Chinese, China launched a limited invasion of northern Vietnam in February 1979 to 'teach Vietnam a lesson'. As massed columns of Chinese troops moved towards Vietnam's northern cities, hoping to draw regular Vietnamese army troops away from Cambodia and into direct battle, they found themselves fighting battle-hardened reservists resorting to Vietnam War–style guerrilla tactics. Vietnam resolutely kept its regular troops on the ground in Cambodia or massed in defence of Hanoi. Chinese forces were mauled by guerrilla tactics in several desperate battles; having declared the road to Hanoi open, they retreated northwards, razing infrastructure and agriculture behind them.[12]

It was China that learned the lesson of the 1979 border war. Like the United States, it concluded that ideological fervour and armed aggression on the Asian continent sapped military credibility and heightened diplomatic isolation. As he consolidated power in China, Deng focused attention on internal reforms of the Chinese economy, while quietly ending Beijing's support for communist insurgents other than the Khmer Rouge.[13] Vietnam's occupation of Cambodia was unfinished business for Deng, but in supporting the Cambodian rebels, China found itself on the same side as the United States and the non-communist states of Southeast Asia. In settling on a pragmatic accommodation with the United States, China accepted the American security guarantee to the non-communist countries in its neighbourhood, while beginning the painstaking process of normalising relations with governments it formerly sought to undermine.

The Eclipse of Ambition

The 1970s became the decade of reckoning in Asia, the taming of power and ambition by reality. Across the continent, from West to South to Central Asia, seething rivalries settled into stable understandings and balances of forces, while grand ambition slowly bled itself white on debilitating resistance struggles. Pragmatism prevailed over obsession; stability trumped pride. Strategic ambition foundered, while self-limitation brought stability to most, and remarkable prosperity to some.

It began in late 1971, when Indian troops started moving into East Pakistan in response to the millions of refugees streaming across India's borders to escape a brutal crackdown on independence protests. The government in West Pakistan ordered air attacks on Indian air-force installations in northwest India on 3 December, triggering an incisive and carefully calibrated response from New Delhi. In short order Indian forces occupied Dhaka, the capital of East Pakistan, while in the west seizing strategic strongholds in Kashmir and making a thrust into Sindh Province, threatening to cut communications between West Pakistan's biggest cities, Lahore and Karachi. When Indian prime minister Indira Gandhi and Pakistani president Zulfikar Ali Bhutto met in the old colonial retreat of Simla to hammer out a peace agreement, a new balance on the subcontinent had emerged. East Pakistan would secede to become an independent Bangladesh, painfully but decisively ending Pakistan's debilitating division by its greatest rival. Indian troops withdrew from Bangladesh and Sindh but not from their gains in Kashmir, as they had done under pressure from Moscow after the last Indo-Pakistani War in 1965. For India, the war had eased its fears of encirclement – not just by two wings of a hostile Pakistan, but also by China and the United States. Gandhi and her advisers had judged shrewdly that neither of Pakistan's great patrons would or could do much to stop India's limited military operations.[14]

Further west, on Asia's Mediterranean shores, another cathartic conflict was brewing. Anwar al-Sadat succeeded Gamal Abdel Nasser as Egyptian president in September 1970. Inheriting a society seething with resentment and in a desperate economic malaise, Sadat was convinced the ultimate cause lay in the shame of the 1967 defeat at the hands of a much smaller Israeli force. Sadat needed the surge of pride and popularity that would follow a military victory over Israel as a precursor to the drastic and painful reforms that were vital for the economy.[15] Overseeing a massive build-up of Soviet weapons for the Egyptian armed forces, Sadat spoke repeatedly about Egypt's willingness to go to war to restore national pride and reclaim the Sinai territories seized by Israel in the Six Day War. Sadat found common cause with his Syrian counterpart, Hafez al-Asad, who agreed to coordinate with Egypt in an attack on Israeli forces.

On the afternoon of 6 October 1973 – during the festival of Yom Kippur for Jews and Ramadan for Arabs – Egyptian forces streamed through breaches in the Bar-Lev Line, the fortifications built by Israel along the Suez Canal to defend the Sinai territories they occupied. Simultaneously, Syrian artillery and aircraft opened up a barrage against Israeli positions in preparation for the advance of Syrian forces deep into the Golan Heights. Cairo and Damascus had learned the lessons of 1967, when Israeli jets had pulverised Arab armies, this time using Soviet-supplied anti-aircraft missiles to beat back Israeli air strikes. In the north, however, Israeli forces had routed the Syrians, rapidly advancing to within 40 kilometres of Damascus. Fearful of a Syrian collapse followed by the full brunt of Israel's power in the Sinai, Sadat gambled on a renewed eastward thrust by Egyptian forces, taking them out from under the protective cover of his anti-aircraft missiles. The Israelis pounced on a gap between Egypt's second and third armies, sending forces across to the western bank of the Suez Canal and quickly encircling the Egyptian third army.[16]

By this stage, the fourth Arab-Israeli War was threatening to blow up into a superpower confrontation. On 25 October, the Soviet president Leonid Brezhnev appealed to the United States to join it and compel the combatants to observe a rapidly unravelling UN-mandated ceasefire or risk the Soviet Union intervening unilaterally to relieve the beleaguered Egyptian forces. Washington put its forces on nuclear alert, warning Egypt that if Moscow intervened on its side, America would intervene to support Israel. Other Arab states, furious at the American support for Israel, announced an oil embargo, quadrupling the price of oil and sending the world economy into a prolonged recession. The October War shattered Israel's belief that it could effortlessly and relatively costlessly defend itself from its Arab neighbours. Post-mortems in Israel revealed failures in intelligence, policymaking and strategy. While the war restored Arab pride somewhat, it also underlined to Israel's antagonists the futility of a conventional military solution to the conflict. Out of the carnage and desperation of the October War came the Israeli-Egyptian peace agreement of 17 September 1978, whereby Israel withdrew its forces from the Sinai and Egypt recognised Israel's right to exist.

Two short wars – one in South Asia, one in West Asia – had brought new stability to postcolonial partition conflicts that had festered for three decades. The superpowers, shocked at how close the October 1973 war had brought them to a nuclear confrontation, redoubled their efforts towards détente. It was to be not détente but Islamic fervour and resistance that would tame the power and ambition of the other major threat to Asian stability: the Soviet Union.

Few in the Kremlin noticed when large demonstrations began in the Iranian capital following the death of the son of an exiled religious leader, Ruhollah Khomeini, in October 1977. The shah of Iran, an American ally, had faced sporadic outbreaks of protest for decades from a society scandalised by the liberation of women, redistribution of agricultural land, rampant inflation, widespread corruption and promotion of western tastes and lifestyles. Iran's secret police, the SAVAK, had been brutally effective at cowing roiling social resentment for a quarter of a century. But the demonstrations continued to build and spread to most of the country's major cities, particularly after protesters were killed by security forces; by mid-1978 there were hundreds of thousands on the streets.[17] By October a general strike had paralysed the economy and by December millions were protesting. The shah, dying of cancer, fled the United States in January 1979. The revolution grew increasingly radical and dominated by conservative religious leaders led by the returned Khomeini. Iran became a theocracy, bent on exporting its model of rule by clerics to the rest of the Muslim world.

By this stage, the Kremlin was taking notice. While many Soviet policymakers rejoiced in the overthrow of an American ally who had allowed listening stations all along the Iranian-Soviet border, others worried about what it would mean for the stability of the majority-Muslim republics in Soviet Central Asia. These concerns became more pressing when a rebellion broke out in the province of Herat in Afghanistan, just across the border from Iran. Moscow was the major backer of the government of Afghanistan, which had come to power in a socialist coup in March 1978, and wasted little time in forcing reforms in agriculture, education and women's rights on a traditional society. The Kremlin initially rebuffed the Afghan government's appeals for assistance as the Islamic revolt against the reforms spread from Herat. Soviet premier Alexei Kosygin argued that Soviet intervention would face substantial domestic and international opposition. But another coup in Kabul, replacing a Soviet-aligned leader with an American-leaning one, raised fears of American troops and listening posts on the Soviet Union's vulnerable southern border. On Christmas Eve 1979, the Soviet 40th Army began streaming over the border into Afghanistan.[18]

The consequences were even worse than Kosygin had painted in his opposition to the invasion. International condemnation was swift and harsh, including from erstwhile allies such as Romania and India. Détente was dead, as a new, assertive Republican White House assailed Soviet interests and legitimacy. Sixty-five countries boycotted the 1980 Moscow Summer Olympics. Instead of damping down Islamic rage across its southern borders, the Afghan insurgency attracted money and recruits from across the Muslim world, including many in the regions of Chechnya and Dagestan, which would explode in rebellion against Moscow after the Soviet collapse. Although Soviet casualties were just over a quarter of those lost by the United States in Vietnam, the war was highly corrosive to the Kremlin's crumbling legitimacy, as the number of dead and maimed rose in a conflict that was seldom mentioned officially and that few sons of the *nomenklatura* were sent to. An even greater toll was exacted on the stalling Soviet economy, ill prepared to fund a grinding war amid falling oil prices.

The invasion of Afghanistan punctured Soviet ambition in Asia. Although the Kremlin made much of the power of the Soviet Pacific fleet, Moscow's attention and resources were drawn away from East and West Asia and increasingly focused on the festering war on its southern borders. The Soviet threat to China's borders became less daunting, while Soviet allies such as Vietnam seemed both less sure of themselves and, in Vietnam's case, trapped in its own Afghanistan in Cambodia. When Mikhail Gorbachev came to power in 1986, he immediately set about building rapprochement with the Soviet Union's neighbours in Asia.[19] The Red Army began to withdraw from Afghanistan, and Vietnamese troops from Cambodia in 1989. Soon after, the Soviet Union peacefully imploded.

The Grounds of Prosperity

Out of a decade of bloodshed arose a new era in Asia. Conflict hadn't been banished – thousands more were to die in the Cambodian jungles, the Hindu Kush, the sands of the Persian Gulf and the shores of the Mediterranean by century's end – but the belief that war, insurgency and ideological conquest could decisively reshape Asia to the benefit of some and disadvantage of others had lost all currency. In its place arose a new spirit of pragmatism. As Beijing and Washington established a new and practical relationship, China gained its seat at the United Nations and quickly established diplomatic relations with Japan, Malaysia, Thailand, Australia and New Zealand. Deng Xiaoping ended the era in which China concentrated on exporting revolution, and began reforms that would make China the world's largest exporter of consumer goods. In the spring of 1972, the leaders of North and South Korea exchanged secret emissaries after twenty years of virtual war and mutual vitriol, culminating in a joint statement in July pledging to seek unification by 'independent means' without 'external interference'.[20] At a leaders' summit in Bali in February 1976, the five non-communist countries of Southeast Asia signed a Treaty of Amity and Cooperation, agreeing to shelve their rivalries and disputes to concentrate on building stability and prosperity in their countries and more broadly across Southeast Asia.

Few could have predicted the developmental effects of the new era of peace and pragmatism in Asia. The Swedish economist Gunnar Myrdal, awarded the 1974 Nobel Prize in Economics, had made a gloomy assessment of Asia's prospects in his three-volume study *Asian Drama: An Inquiry Into the Poverty of Nations*. Myrdal believed that tradition was too strong and governments too 'soft' to allow the major social and policy changes necessary to bring about economic development.[21] Once required reading for development economists, *Asian Drama* is now largely forgotten – because it was soon proved to be spectacularly wrong. Between 1975 and 2000 – the last quarter of the twentieth century – most of the countries of Asia grew strongly, and a smaller subset experienced the fastest economic development the world had ever seen. The average growth rates across the countries of Asia's Pacific Rim easily outstripped those of any other of the world's regions – doubling the growth rates of the developed world and tripling those of Latin America, South Asia and the Middle East. In its landmark 1993 report hailing East Asia's economic miracle, the World Bank wrote, 'if growth were randomly distributed [among the world's countries], there is roughly one chance in ten thousand that [East Asian countries'] success would have been so regionally concentrated'.[22]

The coming of prosperity to Asia was unprecedented in pace, scale and quality. While it took Britain fifty-eight years and America fifty to double their income through industrialisation, it took the countries of Northeast Asia an average of 7.6 years to double their income after 1975. Southeast Asia and South Asia took slightly longer to do the same thing – around 9.5 years. By the end of the twentieth century, China's economy had grown by a factor of five, as had Thailand's and Malaysia's; Korea's by a factor of nine; Taiwan's by twelve; Singapore's by thirteen; and India's had tripled in size. In 1975 the average income of Koreans was similar to that of Papua New Guineans; by 2000 it was slightly more than the average income in the Netherlands.[23]

This extraordinary period of development had occurred in countries comprising over half of the world's population. The result was the most rapid reduction of global poverty in history. In 1975, 57.7 per cent of the population of Northeast Asia lived below the poverty line; in twenty years that proportion had fallen to 21.2 per cent. China alone lifted 400 million people out of poverty during the last quarter of the twentieth century.[24] And remarkably, all but a handful of these countries achieved this rapid economic growth while maintaining and even improving their rates of economic equality.

Thousands of books, articles and reports have been written about the causes of Asia's remarkable economic performance in the fourth quarter of the twentieth century. Debates have raged over the economic 'formulas' that Asian states used to drive such rapid industrialisation and over the policy frameworks that governments used to foster economic growth. But while particular economic formulas and policy frameworks may well have been the *sufficient* causes of Asia's economic growth, they could not have worked without the *necessary* conditions of Asia's success – the underlying factors which, had they been absent, would have condemned Asia to the relative economic stagnation it had seen in the twentieth century's first three quarters. It was the taming of power politics, the sublimation of rivalry and a focus on collective and individual development that provided the space for Asia's particular economic formulas and policy frameworks to begin the work their particular magic. The necessary conditions of Asia's peace and prosperity in the fourth quarter of the twentieth century were provided by three interlocking pillars.

The first pillar was a relatively 'flat' topography of power across the continent – meaning that no country felt itself to be large or wealthy or internally strong enough to aspire to dominance in its region. In large part this was the result of the decade of reckoning that was the 1970s: the humbling of strategic ambition and ideological zeal across the continent of Asia. The costs of adventurism and war had proved far too high, while the benefits of compromise and self-limitation seemed to mount with each passing year. Asia certainly contained some big countries – the world's biggest in fact, by population and size – but these were too poor and too internally divided to realistically contemplate any sort of dominance. The two superpowers, which had regarded Asia and Europe as the key to the cosmic struggle between capitalism and communism, each found themselves humbled by grinding guerrilla wars in Asia. Asia also had some of the world's wealthiest countries – and as the quarter century of peace passed, increasingly so – but Singapore, Taiwan, Hong Kong, the United Arab Emirates and Qatar were too small to turn their wealth into strategic power. Although it was the wealthiest – and reasonably large and certainly unified, Japan was, if anything, the most timid, weighed down by war memories, a pacifist constitution and a client-like alliance with the United States.

The fact that no country in Asia felt large, wealthy and internally strong enough to contemplate regional dominance meant that most countries could relax, comparatively. For almost all – Israel at one end of Asia and Taiwan at the other stand out as obvious exceptions – worries about internal security easily trumped their concerns about external security. Many of the continent's security forces were consciously shaped to play internal roles: fighting subversion and terrorism, forestalling secessionist movements, controlling inter-ethnic tensions. The focus on internal security showed Asia's states that they had much more in common in the security realm than had been apparent during earlier periods of tension and conflict among them.

The second pillar supporting Asia's peace arose from, and supported, the first. It was a belief among an increasing number of the region's elites that economic development and stability were more important than any other consideration. At a meeting in Bangkok in August 1967, the foreign ministers of Southeast Asia's five non-communist states agreed to form a regional organisation called the Association of Southeast Asian Nations (ASEAN). At the core of the new body was a collective commitment that no political, territorial, ethnic or ideological dispute should be allowed to threaten the stability and development of all. Each of the five – Indonesia, Singapore, Malaysia, Thailand and the Philippines – realised that to achieve resilience and development inside their borders, they needed collectively to foster resilience and development in their broader region. They also agreed that by shelving their disputes and rivalries and focusing on development, they would remove the temptation for larger powers to intervene in Southeast Asia. The essence of ASEAN became a belief that stability fosters development and development fosters stability.[25]

At the time, few external observers took much notice of ASEAN. None of the frictions, territorial disputes and deep rivalries among the five had been resolved – they had merely been shelved. What's more, previous attempts to form a regional body in Southeast Asia had soon foundered on these shoals. But ASEAN endured, each year recommitting to its mutual stability and development pact. As it neared its tenth anniversary, a growing number of countries and organisations had applied and been granted the status of dialogue partners: Australia, Japan, New Zealand, the United States, Canada, the European Community and the United Nations Development Program. ASEAN's success radiated outwards, drawing in five more Southeast Asian countries as they gained independence (Brunei), opened up (Myanmar), ended conflicts (Vietnam, Cambodia) or bid farewell to Cold War tensions (Laos). By the 1990s, as new, broader institutions evolved in Asia, ASEAN was placed firmly at their core, injecting the philosophy of stability, development and mutual respect into their every sinew, ultimately drawing in all of the region's big powers – China, Japan, India, the United States, Russia.[26]

The third pillar underpinning Asia's stability and development was a network of mutually supporting economic and security relationships. After the Second World War, the United States had anchored its presence across the Pacific by way of a system of alliances: with Japan, Korea, Taiwan, the Philippines, South Vietnam, Thailand, Australia and New Zealand. Some security commitments had also spread among American allies, through the short-lived Southeast Asia Treaty Organization, or among the British Commonwealth countries – Britain, Malaysia, Singapore, Australia and New Zealand – which signed the Five Power Defence Arrangements in November 1971. These Pacific alliances were nothing like those that spanned the Atlantic Ocean, where the North Atlantic Treaty Organization saw the heavy concentration of American forces in Europe and the substantial integration of weapons and command structures among the allies. The only American troops stationed in Asia were in Japan and Korea; the other alliances were looser, and formed around basing and intelligence relationships.

The 'alliance-lite' model worked perfectly in Asia, where even staunchly non-aligned countries accepted the benefits of the largely benign and distracted American security presence in their part of the Pacific. Singaporean prime minister Goh Chok Tong captured the mood perfectly in 2000 when he said:

> There is a grudging acceptance that the US continues to be a stabilizing factor in the region. While there are differences in how each ASEAN country sees the US security presence, there is an underlying recognition that without it, the politics of the region would be more complex and troublesome.[27]

America's benign and distracted attitude towards its Pacific alliances was complemented by its tolerant attitude to the ways non-communist Asian states organised their affairs. In ways Washington would never have tolerated in Europe, most of the states of Pacific Asia instituted soft authoritarian rule aligned with state involvement in the economy, designed to concentrate and mobilise domestic wealth and expertise, shut out external competitors and shut down internal critics and labour unions. The United States economy was opened to the import of manufactures from Asian economies that were kept resolutely closed to reciprocal trade. Asia's non-communist economies developed quickly on the back of intensive exports of consumer goods made highly competitive by rigid control of labour and capital costs and closely managed exchange rates.

Around the Pacific Ocean rim there developed a trading and investment cycle linking together the remarkable complementarities among North American consumers, Northeast Asian manufacturing, cheap Southeast Asian labour and Australian minerals and energy. This dynamic economic network compensated for the separation of Asia's Pacific economies from their traditional hinterland in the Asian continent by the Communist victory in China and the deepening hostility of the Cold War. Until the opening up of Asia's communist economies in the 1980s and 1990s, the non-communist Pacific Rim easily outpaced the closed economies of the Asian mainland.[28]

The alignment of security commitments and economic partnerships created a positive spiral. Even in the face of mounting trade deficits, the United States kept its markets open to Asian exports because it knew that the rapid growth in wealth of its Pacific allies would ultimately strengthen them against communist aggression, both domestic and external. The American security presence in the Pacific provided a reassuring cushion that allowed Asia's non-communist states to underspend on external defence and maximise investment in their booming manufacturing sectors. The rising wealth of their societies disinclined Asian countries to take issue with the irritations and ignominies of being part of the 'free world' – the seigniorial privileges Washington enjoyed with the greenback as the sole trading currency, the dominance of global institutions by America and Europe, the uncomfortable compromises the United States occasionally foisted on them. On the other hand, the compliance and stability of the societies of the Pacific Rim made it easier for Washington to overlook their less-than-liberal governance and economic policies. By the late 1990s, it was broadly accepted that the next century would be the Asia–Pacific one.

The Future of Peace

How long will Asia's peace and prosperity endure? Will the patterns of pragmatic stability and reinforcing economic growth established in the last quarter of the twentieth century persist in the twenty-first? There is no shortage of prestigious predictions that Asia's peace and prosperity will continue. 'An economic renaissance is unfolding in the region,' write two World Bank economists, '[a]t current growth trends, East Asia will be as large in terms of the world economy (40 per cent) by 2025 as it was in 1820, around the time it began a long decline in global importance.'[29] Research from HSBC Banking Group forecasts that ten of the twenty-six 'fast growth' economies in the world to 2050 will be in Asia;[30] Citigroup lists nine of its eleven 'global growth generators' to 2050 in Asia;[31] while Goldman Sachs continues to list Asian powerhouses among its future global growth drivers.[32] 'The transformation of the Asian region into the economic powerhouse of the world is not only unstoppable, it is gathering pace,' writes an Australian government report.[33] The rise of Asia, writes prominent Singaporean commentator Kishore Mahbubani, means 'the world as a whole will become more peaceful and stable'.[34]

If a flat power topography, the subordination of rivalry to development and alignment of security and prosperity dynamics were the necessary conditions for Asia's late-twentieth-century transformation, it is worth asking whether these three pillars remain unchanged. Seen in historical terms, the first – the region's flat power topography – would appear to be an extremely unstable pillar. If, in 1975, no Asian country appeared large or wealthy or internally strong enough to aspire to dominance in its region, this condition looks increasingly questionable today. China's potential – for so long just potential – looks much more like reality today. It is second only to the United States in economic size and military spending, with population and geographic expanse that are continental in scope. Thirty-five years after the turmoil of Mao's succession and twenty-five after Tiananmen Square, the Chinese Communist Party has just managed its third seamless leadership transition. Whether China *aspires* to regional leadership is immaterial – the key issue for the region's power topography is that other countries can *imagine* it doing so. This fact alone has been enough to drive hedging moves among most of China's neighbours, meaning that as they integrate ever more closely with China's economy, they are reaching out to each other and the United States to balance China's growing weight and influence. China is not alone in its growing wealth, power and ambition. Many of its neighbours, partly due to their own development and partly in response to China's rise, are gaining strength and ambition. The topography of power in Asia now looks more like a pyramid than a billiard table.

The second pillar, the absolute subordination of rivalries and ambitions to the goal of development, is also starting to wobble. Nearly forty years of barely interrupted growth has made the aversion to poverty more remote and brought the temptation of strengthening military capabilities closer. Territorial disputes, once cautiously tiptoed around, have begun to heat up across Asia. As Asian states become less worried about internal stability, they have been freed to focus their anxieties and ambitions outwards, and as they gain in strength and confidence, unresolved territorial disagreements seem less and less acceptable. From west to east, Asia has become the area of largest growth in arms sales. And the arming of Asia has extended into the nuclear realm. Just before the turn of the millennium, India and Pakistan crossed the threshold to nuclear weapons status and North Korea shortly afterwards, and there is every likelihood Iran will reach that point by 2025. Japan remains a nuclear threshold state, with the fissile material and know-how to develop nuclear weapons very quickly, while both the Republic of Korea and Taiwan have shown an interest in nuclear enrichment in recent decades. As the 1970s, the decade of reckoning in Asia, recedes into the past, force as a policy option is creeping back.

The third pillar, the close alignment of security commitments and economic relationships, has completely crumbled. The opening of the Chinese economy has re-established the Asian mainland as the economic hinterland of Asia's Pacific economies. Today all but a handful have China as their major trading partner and those that don't, list China in their top five. Many have China in their top five investment relationships also. But as they have integrated economically with China, many have simultaneously tightened their security relations with the United States. This includes Vietnam, a country that was at war with America a generation ago. The bifurcation of security and economic interests is now a reality from Japan to Australia to India, and for many countries in between. Thus far, most countries have struck a balance between their economic and security interests, but in the context of deepening rivalry between the United States and China such choices will be harder and harder to manage.

What will Asia's coming century look like, given the three necessary conditions for its stability and prosperity during the late twentieth century have eroded? Has the continent's prosperity gained such momentum, its habits of accommodation and stability become so ingrained that we can look forward to more of the same? Or have we crossed a threshold without noticing, into a new era of conflict and rivalry? It's time to look at Asia's current defining trends, and ponder where they may interact and shape this great continent – and ultimately the world.

2

SIGNIFICANT OTHERS

The little village of Kibithu is the easternmost settlement in India and easily one of the most spectacular. Located in the snow-capped eastern Himalayas of Arunachal Pradesh state, it is couched in lush forests traversed by rushing rivulets and waterfalls. Where these rivers of melting snow cut through mountain ramparts has long been a highway of civilisations. Through these passes, Buddhist teachings made their way from India into Tibet, China and Burma. Silver and spices were brought up Burma's Irrawaddy River, bound through the mountain passes for China and India. These were the courses along which the preparation and cultivation of tea emanated from China into British India and Burma.

Kibithu lies close to the point where Indian, Chinese and Burmese territory meets. It is part of the 65,000 kilometres of territory claimed by Beijing as part of the Tibetan Autonomous Region. Kibithu was subject to a ferocious battle between Chinese and Indian forces in October 1962, and was briefly occupied by the People's Liberation Army before it withdrew across the 'Line of Actual Control' – the ostensible but disputed boundary between India and China. The Line of Actual Control follows quite closely the border drawn up under the supervision of Sir Henry McMahon, the foreign secretary of the British Raj in India, who oversaw a boundary convention in the colonial hill station of Simla in mid-1914. The Simla Convention had been convened to find a solution to the problem caused when Tibetans had evicted Chinese troops and officials after the collapse of the last dynasty in Beijing in 1911.[1] The negotiations in Simla divided the eastern Himalayas into 'inner Tibet', to remain part of British India, and 'outer Tibet', with nominal independence under Chinese suzerainty. The British and Tibetan representatives in Simla signed the agreement but not the Chinese. The McMahon Line became part of the independence settlement, as Britain dismantled the raj after the end of the Second World War. When inner Tibet became part of independent India in 1947, the Tibetan government tendered a note to the new government in New Delhi claiming large parts of the region. On gaining power in 1949, the Chinese Communist Party repudiated the McMahon Line on the grounds that the Tibetans had no right to conclude a boundary treaty in 1914, and declared its intention to liberate inner Tibet.

India and China are not the only parties disputing the easternmost parts of Arunachal Pradesh. The region is also home to tribal militias who call themselves the 'Naga peoples' and identify more strongly with kin across the border in today's Myanmar than with Indians or Chinese. A long-running insurgency has plagued the region and the Indian government since the 1970s. But for the arbitrary border drawn between India, China and Burma by the British Empire in 1937, the Naga peoples could have been living alongside their ethnic kin in Myanmar – or instead of fighting Indian troops, they could be battling China's People's Liberation Army.[2]

By such quirks of history, Kibithu is part of India and therefore classified as part of 'South Asia' or the 'subcontinent'. Both these labels carry loaded connotations: chronic poverty and underdevelopment, 'Hindu rates of growth', overcrowding and poor sanitation, vast inert bureaucracies, and almost constant instability and conflict. But had

British geographers decided to place Kibithu in Burma rather than India, it would have been part of Southeast Asia, not South Asia. Automatically it would have been part of a different system of classification, implying that it belonged to a society that was stable, ordered and ruled by technocratic (though not necessarily democratic) government, promoting rapid economic development. Or if the People's Liberation Army had not withdrawn in 1963, Kibithu would today have been part of China and therefore Northeast Asia, an even more prestigious club still: of industrial power, high-tech cities, gleaming infrastructure, 'Confucian' discipline and control.

Conquer and Divide

Dividing the world's largest, most populous and most diverse continent into arbitrary chunks is a very old habit of the human mind. Geographers tell us that to understand and navigate the world, we need to divide and order it according to shared 'mental maps'. Asia's great expanse and diversity seems too great for the mind to encompass and comprehend all at once; it seems natural to divide it into sub-regions in order to focus in and understand it properly. But for much of the past half millennium, Asia was divided for more than simple taxonomic reasons. The great wealth of the Asian continent was far too alluring to the kingdoms and republics of Europe to rely on simple trade flows. Treasure and power would flow to those that could carve out exclusive empires in Asia, bringing to an end the flows of east–west trade and establishing absolute colonial enclaves between the metropole in Europe and its imperial territories in Asia. In the process, a continent once responsible for close to 70 per cent of all economic activity on earth was reduced to a series of peripheral appendages of European empires, connected more vitally to the metropole and its other colonies than to other Asian economies.

The ancient Greeks were the first to call the vast continent to their east by a single name, Ἀσία, which they distinguished from their own Europe and from Africa to their south. The pre-colonial empires and kingdoms that inhabited the Asian continent occupied distinct and largely self-contained spaces, often separated from each other by mountains, seas or deserts. War, trade and religion maintained regular exchanges and influences across the vast continent. Beliefs, techniques, spices and knowledge were remarkably portable among Asia's diverse societies and, for the most part, those societies proved strongly absorbent of outside influences. A flexible pragmatism seemed to govern the interplay of cultures: whether the imported beliefs were Hindu concepts of governance, or Chinese characters, or Malay standards of commerce, or Buddhist moral codes or Arabic mathematics, the recipient cultures adapted them to their own needs while maintaining their own distinctive cultural traditions.[3] Pilgrimage, commerce and alliances forged human diasporas and networks along Asia's trading routes, while a tolerance for difference resulted in richly complex mixes of culture and religion in many of Asia's societies.

The first time the diverse peoples of the continent called Asia were given a sense of their common geography came at the end of the thirteenth century, when the vast empire of Genghis Khan stretched from southern China into central Europe, creating the conditions for the flourishing of the Silk Road.[4] Far to the south, along the Indian Ocean and western Pacific sea lanes, the continent's other great trading highway emerged, linking three commercial zones. Demarcated by proximity and monsoonal rhythms, the great trading route from the islands of Japan to the Persian Gulf was divided into three circuits centred on the Arabian Sea, the Bay of Bengal and the South China Sea, plied by Arab, Indian and Malay and Chinese merchants respectively. At the great trading ports of Melaka, Calicut and Hormuz, cargoes were exchanged between Arab, Indian and Malay and Chinese merchants for the next leg of the voyage.[5]

These traditions of easy interpenetration did not reach beyond the shores of the Mediterranean. European society was neither open to new and diverse influences nor tolerant of heterogeneity. Christendom had split into acrimoniously competing eastern and western variants; western Christendom would soon fracture further, leading to vicious sectarian warfare. Unlike in Asia, territory in Europe was strictly divided and jealously exclusive. Territorial divisions became the basis for religion and belief, and minorities were regularly persecuted and driven out. And unlike the easy exchanges and collaborations across Asia's terrestrial and maritime silk roads, commerce in Europe was brutally competitive.

Ironically, it was trade with Asia that drove commercial warfare in Europe. Capturing the wealth of the Asia trade was an alluring prize to European states gripped by the spiralling costs of a new age of warfare, brought about by the gunpowder revolution. As the costs of war outstripped tax revenues, kings and republics alike began to see the revenues from trade as a matter of life and death. Unlike the Ottoman, Mughal or Ming empires in Asia, the kingdoms and republics of Europe saw no distinction between commerce and politics, or merchants and warriors. As early as 1506, 27 per cent of the income of the king of Portugal came from the spice trade; by 1518 it was 39 per cent – greater than the taxation income of the crown. Over half of the revenue flowing to Henry VI of England came from customs duties.[6] The logic was inescapable. The more commercial revenue that could be captured by Europe's monarchs and republics, to the exclusion of their competitors, the stronger the prospects for survival of the realm. The smaller the realm, the more urgently it needed commercial revenue.[7]

Commercial warfare was most intense in the eastern Mediterranean, where Asia's two silk roads converged to service Europe's insatiable demand for spices, porcelain, incense and silk. Byzantium,

Venice, Genoa and Frankish Sicily fought to dominate the shores, islands and maritime straits of the eastern Mediterranean; by the end of the fourteenth century, through brutality and guile, the Venetians had prevailed. With the naval might of Venice holding the eastern Mediterranean, an increasingly desperate search began for an alternative route to the riches of Asia. The courts of Spain and Portugal were the most vigorous at first, and their competition was fierce. In 1481, the Portuguese secured a papal bull, *Æterni regis*, granting all lands, discovered and undiscovered, south of the Canary Islands to Portugal. The Spanish, unwilling to allow Columbus's discoveries to be allocated to Lisbon, capitalised on Pope Alexander VI's Spanish blood to secure another bull, *Inter caetera*, in 1493, granting Spain all lands west and south of the longitude 100 leagues west of the Cape Verde islands. The following year, in 1494, Spain and Portugal divided the world outside Europe between them by the Treaty of Tordesillas.

Accordingly, Vasco da Gama, who rounded the southern tip of Africa and sailed to India in 1497, regarded the Indian Ocean as a Portuguese lake – as did the Portuguese captains who followed him. Their king, Manuel I, had styled himself 'King of Portugal and Algarves of either side of the sea in Africa, Lord of Guinea and of the Conquest, Navigation and Commerce of Ethiopia, Arabia, Persia and India'. The Portuguese aim was not to compete with the Venetians in the Asia trade, but to seize it from them – and the Arabs, Indians, Malays and Chinese.[8] In effect, the Portuguese copied Venice's model of armed trade monopoly in the Mediterranean and applied it to the Indian Ocean. Lisbon's empire became a vast and brutal protection racket. Portuguese warships seized strategic ports, including Goa, Cochin, Colombo, Malacca and Macao, from which they patrolled the sea lanes of the Indian Ocean. Any non-Portuguese ship found to be without a *cartaz* – a permission note obliging it to call at Portuguese ports and pay customs duties – was attacked and sunk. The Portuguese crown established a monopoly over the Indian Ocean spice trade to keep prices high and competitors out.[9] At the height of the Portuguese empire, Tomé Pires, a Portuguese apothecary-turned-diplomat, mused: 'just as doors are the defence of houses, so seaports are the help, defence and main protection of provinces and kingdoms . . . whoever is lord of Melaka has his hand on the throat of Venice'.[10]

But soon powerful predators appeared. Ill-advisedly, the Portuguese had begun to hand over the distribution of their spice trade in northern Europe to the Dutch. These dour, calculating Protestants had a keen nose for opportunities to expand their trade and transport businesses. They had also thrown off the rule of Europe's superpower of the time, imperial Spain. When the Spanish king Phillip II acceded to the Portuguese throne in 1580, the Dutch flipped from being distributors for the Portuguese empire to direct competitors. A Dutchman named Jan Huyghen van Linschoten chose his nationality over his religion (he was a Catholic like Phillip II, unlike most Dutch) and passed on the knowledge he had gained from years working in the east to his compatriots. A very large island called Java, rich in spices and open to conquest, could be reached without sailing through the waters patrolled by Iberian gunships – if the Dutch were prepared to brave the open ocean.[11]

Fortified by their Protestant faith in a direct relationship with God, the Dutch were prepared to take greater risks than the Portuguese, whose carracks hugged Africa's and Asia's coasts and monsoon highways. A ship that sailed directly east after rounding Africa's southern tip soon found itself driven hard by a constant westerly wind, whipped up by a stream of warm air from the Equator meeting the earth's rotation and unmediated by any baffling landmass. Dutch merchants skimmed across the Indian Ocean far south of where they would be asked for *cartazes*, turning north on reaching the vast silent continent of Australia and soon finding themselves in a spice paradise – what is today called Indonesia. The aromatic riches of Java and the Moluccas convinced the burghers of Amsterdam that their control over the spice trade could be as total as that of the Portuguese, whom they would displace. But instead of controlling trade routes, the Dutch decided to control entire commodities, from cultivation through harvest, transportation and distribution. As well as consolidating their control over the Indonesian Spice Islands, the Dutch systematically dismantled the Portuguese protection racket by seizing key ports and shutting down its production and transport operations.[12]

The Dutch protection racket in Asia was as short-lived as that of the Portuguese. Another Protestant maritime people, the English, had tasted the heady promise of trade in the course of its own desperate struggle with imperial Spain. The Dutch were able to eject the English from early footholds in the East Indies but were powerless to stop their accumulation of commercial footholds on the Indian subcontinent and in the Persian Gulf. Soon the Dutch found that the English were strangling their trade monopoly in the same way the Dutch had strangled that of the Portuguese. The English trade protection racket in Asia was different again from those of the Portuguese and Dutch. It was governed by a series of crown privileges, allowing favoured corporations to engage in certain trades to the exclusion of all other competitors as a way of maintaining high crown royalties and eliminating the risk of competition. The overall strategy was to place London at the centre of a trading empire: boosting British industry and exports, maximising the carrying trade in British hulls, strangling competitors and making London the warehouse and clearing house of a global system. The British soon set about dislodging the Dutch, the French and any uncooperative local rulers from ports and coasts that would be vital for British trading monopolies.[13]

So the struggle for national survival in Europe drove a progressive carving up of the riches of Asia. The Spanish and Portuguese, the Dutch and English, and the Russians, French and Germans in effect reproduced in Asia a patchwork of mutually exclusive territories reminiscent of those they had etched across the face of Europe. So important was the Asia trade to national survival that the intensity of the competition among the Europeans became a driver of high imperialism: a need to establish absolute control over lucrative territories and exclude competitors from access to their raw materials and markets; a dread of competitors gaining footholds; and an obsessive urge to expand territorial control to forestall rivals.[14]

The imperial age in Asia brought an end to Asia's silk roads – the generally peaceable commercial highways across which commodities, ideas, people and faiths had flowed relatively seamlessly for centuries. Instead, Asia's diverse societies became locked into a series of mutually exclusive global empires. The territories controlled by the British became more vitally connected with the other parts of the British Empire – in the Americas, Africa and the Pacific – than with Asian societies outside the British Empire. The same was true for Asian societies governed by France, Spain, the Netherlands and Portugal. The flows of commodities, ideas, institutions, faiths and peoples were now imperial; a subdivided Asia became globally integrated but continentally disintegrated.

The result was the distortion of Asia's economies, their progressive marginalisation within the global economy and the withering of the trade between Asian societies. Asia's economies, once proudly self-sufficient and little interested in the outside world, were reduced to appendages of the metropolitan powers. Crops such as indigo, sugar, jute and tea that couldn't be grown in Europe displaced food and other crops in Asian fields; industries such as textiles and metalware that competed with European manufactures withered beneath a flood of imports. When Asian societies had insufficient demand for what Europeans could offer to balance what Europeans wanted from them, products such as opium were aggressively traded to create that balancing demand. The subdivision into colonies and dependencies inaugurated a long era during which the fortunes of the world's largest continent were determined by empires and great powers outside Asia.

Defence and Dislocation

The carving up of Asia into colonies and states between the sixteenth and eighteenth centuries wasn't to be the last time that the world's largest continent was subdivided. As the societies of Asia threw off colonial rule in the twentieth century, many of their independence leaders embraced the doctrine of 'pan-Asianism' – the idea of the essential solidarity of Asian societies. But new mental maps – partly the result of the world's inability to think about Asia in its vast, varied entirety and partly the result of new political imperatives – were to subdivide the continent anew.

The first impulse towards subdivision was regionalism, the intellectual child of the Allies' ordering of the Second World War into separate theatres to better apportion their forces, coordinate their activities and plan and sequence their campaigns. The British established a Southeast Asia military command as a way of coordinating Allied efforts to push back the Japanese advance – the first time the label had been used. After the war, military theatres morphed into subregions for the purposes of joint Allied administration and postwar reconstruction. As economic and political integration underpinned the remarkable recovery of Western Europe from the ravages of war, 'regionalism' caught on as a project in other parts of the world too. Soon the worlds of academia and diplomacy began to reinforce the logic of regionalism, as western universities developed 'area studies' teaching and research clusters, and foreign ministries reorganised along geographic as well as functional lines.[15] The wartime appellation 'Southeast Asia' persisted after the war, soon to be joined by 'Northeast Asia', a convenient label to describe the rapidly industrialising economies of Japan, South Korea, Taiwan and Hong Kong. South Asia and Central Asia were to follow. Further west, the colonial label 'Middle East' maintained primacy over the term 'West Asia'.

At the same time, a third wave of subdivisions was being etched over the map of Asia, arising from the bitter rivalries of the Cold War. The collaboration among the victors of the Second World War soon crumbled into mutual loathing, suspicion and all-out ideological competition. Once again, the subdivision of Asia had its origins in antagonism and mutually exclusive territorial divisions in Europe. As Europe lay in ruins, the implicit understandings hammered out in wartime summits at Tehran and Yalta about a Soviet sphere of influence in Eastern and Central Europe became manifest. In Washington, the 'Containment' doctrine marshalled the resources of the United States and its allies to prevent what they believed was an innate Soviet impulse to break out of the current territorial limits of the communist bloc. This commitment to defend the new territorial status quo was reciprocated in Moscow, where the Soviet Politburo interpreted America's offers of reconstruction aid and calls for free elections as ploys to subvert the new status quo and drive the west's sphere of influence eastwards. With customary rhetorical flourish, Winston Churchill proclaimed the descent of an Iron Curtain dividing Western and Eastern Europe.

These ideological antagonisms soon infected the dynamics of Asia's postwar and postcolonial settlements. A communist movement that few had taken seriously at the start of the war seized power in China, Asia's biggest country and one of the 'four policemen' that Franklin Roosevelt believed would safeguard international peace and security after the war. The 'loss of China' to communism sparked a bitter debate in the United States, and a country that had been passionately anti-imperialist found itself supporting the bids of the European colonialists to retain their empires in Asia. Against

a monolithic and expansionist communist menace, American policymakers began to sketch out a defensive perimeter of containment
in Asia. Secretary of State Dean Acheson drew that line explicitly in
an address to the National Press Club in Washington, DC in January 1950:

> This defensive perimeter runs along the Aleutians to Japan and
> then goes to the Ryukyus ... [and from] the Ryukyus to the
> Philippine islands ... So far as the military security of other
> areas of the Pacific is concerned, it must be clear that no person
> can guarantee these areas from military attack ... Should such
> an attack occur ... the initial reliance must be on the people
> attacked to resist it and then on commitments of the entire civ-
> ilized world under the Charter of the United Nations.[16]

Five months later, North Korean troops invaded South Korea
with the help of Soviet weapons and advisers. Joseph Stalin had
interpreted Acheson's speech as a declaration of Washington's
lack of interest in the fate of Korea. The blood-drenched war that
followed confirmed the American belief in communism's innate
expansionism and reinforced America's determination to defend
the borders of the free world wherever they lay in Asia. Stalemate delivered a de facto demarcation with communism at the
38th parallel in Korea, but within two years a new confrontation
had emerged, thousands of miles to the south, on the 17th parallel
dividing communist North Vietnam from nationalist South Vietnam. The American defensive perimeter moved onto the Asian
mainland: along the 38th parallel, into the jungles of Vietnam and
onto the military bases of northern Thailand.

Absolute ideological division settled over Asia. It divided
countries: Korea, China and, for a while, Vietnam; it polarised
neighbours and fuelled bitter insurgencies. Despite Sino-Soviet

rivalry, communist Asia was cut off from non-communist Asia and integrated with the rest of the communist world through trade, investment, educational exchanges, arms and technology transfers, and diplomatic alignments. Non-communist Asia drew together in solidarity against communist aggression from without and subversion from within. Pan-Asian sentiment, manifested in the Non-Aligned Movement – a collection of developing countries that rejected the Cold War's polarising alliances – fell prey to intramural squabbles and accusations of bad faith. Those who tried to maintain equidistance between the camps, such as Indonesian president Sukarno, lost control to a military coup that brought a staunchly anti-communist New Order regime to power. Other attempts at non-alignment foundered as Cold War tensions spilled into local conflicts, and countries such as India gravitated towards either the west or the Soviet bloc. Fear of the other side drove the consolidation of authoritarian regimes and ideological zealotry in both communist and non-communist countries.

From colonial land grabs to ideological antagonism and subregions, the successive divisions of Asia originated from beyond the continent. But the motivations for these divisions were adopted and internalised by Asian societies themselves. As decolonisation proceeded across the continent, Asia's newly independent states not only took up the absolute boundary demarcations the imperialists had imposed, but also invested them with a deep significance and defended them with passionate fervour. Unresolved boundary disputes led to ongoing tension, dangerous brinkmanship and repeated conflict in Asia as on no other continent on earth. Asia remains home to two of the world's three surviving Cold War standoffs – the Korean Peninsula and the Taiwan Straits (the third being the hostility between the United States and Cuba). The bitter humiliation of colonial rule or fiat also led to the passionate embrace of the western concept of sovereignty by Asian countries at a time when western states were beginning to abandon their attachment to the concept. From the beginning, Asian governments were hypersensitive to any form of external criticism or interference, as well as deeply intolerant of internal criticism. Societies that had just wrested their independence from colonial overlords were stubbornly unprepared to cede any initiative or control to international institutions, whether regional or global.

Many of Asia's newly independent states were also determined to avoid replacing a system of colonial economic exploitation with one of postcolonial exploitation. The drive to modernise led governments to impose tight restrictions on foreign trade and investment, and to invest heavily in import-substituting industries. By 1970, imports comprised just 2.7 per cent of China's economy, 3.9 per cent of India's, 9.6 per cent of Japan's, 15 per cent of Indonesia's and 19.4 per cent of Thailand's.[17] Locals and visitors had to be contented with 'Thumbs Up' cola in India, 'Long March' toilet paper in China and 'Darkie' toothpaste in Thailand. Global and regional moves towards trade or investment integration were kept at arm's length. When, in 1976, the members of ASEAN decided to push forward regional economic integration by inviting members to nominate sectors of their economies to be liberalised, Indonesia announced it would dramatically slash tariff barriers on snowploughs. By the start of the 1990s, trade among the countries of ASEAN stood at less than 20 per cent of their combined gross domestic products.[18]

Consequential Connections

The coming of stability and prosperity to Asia in the last quarter of the twentieth century unleashed an array of forces that have begun to dissolve the motives and rationales for subdivision, and to drive the reintegration of Asia, from the Pacific to the Mediterranean, from the Arctic to the Indian Ocean. Sovereignty is as keenly held as ever, and subregional labels are still widely used, but in many ways the transnational connections among Asian countries are becoming equally as or more significant than their individual connections with non-Asian countries and regions. Pan-Asian interconnections are rising and thickening, in trade and investment, industry and services, regional organisations, flows of people and mindsets. As these connections grow, they are becoming more consequential: Asian states have a greater and greater stake in each other's success, even as competition and rivalry among them grows. The reintegration of Asia is an event of millennial significance: it heralds a new age in which the most consequential dynamics in the world – be they commercial, ideational, strategic or social – will once again occur on the world's largest continent, and these dynamics will affect the problems and possibilities of the rest of the world.

The roots of Asia's reconnections lie more than a century in its past, ironically at the time of its most abject subjection and division at the hands of high imperialism. In the late nineteenth century, Japan responded the fastest and most vigorously to the challenge of western imperialism because it very quickly found a balance among three possible responses to the west: rejection, emulation and confrontation. At the heart of the Meiji Restoration was a realisation that unless Japan adopted the techniques underpinning western dominance and used them to confront the urges of high imperialism, it would soon be colonised. But balancing these responses was a determination to retain the authenticity of Japanese culture, continuity with Japanese traditions and pride in Japanese values. And so Japanese society became a vanguard for interpreting the techniques and terminologies of western modernisation in terms of classical East Asian concepts. Many of these classical concepts had originated in ancient China and, as they were re-exported to China and Korea, they provided conceptual handles for responding to the challenge of the west, while at the same time maintaining continuity with the classical traditions of these Asian societies. Japan became a hub for intellectuals from a wide array of Asian societies grappling with the challenge of how to respond to western dominance while maintaining cultural authenticity and pride.[19] An awareness began to spread of the common predicament of Asian societies in the age of imperialism, accompanied by a belief in the commonalities among Asian societies and the value of solidarity and cooperation.

To Asia's tragic cost, Japan's reaction to the west soon stretched to the logic of high imperialism and direct confrontation leading to war. Ideals of pan-Asian solidarity became justifications for Japanese colonialism under the guise of an anti-imperialist drive to eject the west from Asia. In Taiwan, Tokyo's first colony, imperial Japan embarked on an experiment with enduring results. When Goto Shimpei took over as colonial governor of Taiwan in 1898, he inaugurated a program that he labelled 'scientific colonialism'. So began an approach that distinguished Japanese from western colonialism: the administration of colonies as laboratories for the technocratic planning of economies and societies, based on the experiences of Japan after the Meiji Restoration. Programs aimed at the wholesale reconstitution of colonised societies in Taiwan, Korea and Manchuria ensued, encompassing urban planning; public hygiene systems; transport, water, communications and energy infrastructure; and widespread public education.[20] Inspired by the ideal of 'constructing East Asia', thousands of young Japanese engineers poured into Japan's colonies, their efforts often welcomed by local elites who had pioneered efforts to modernise their societies before the Japanese arrived.[21]

On these foundations of infrastructure, planning and education, imperial Japan drove forward the industrialisation of its colonies. Its motives were entirely selfish – bolstering the power and self-sufficiency of the Japanese Empire and relieving pressure on Japan's home industry – but the effects were enduring. Not only did colonial and wartime industrialisation accustom Taiwanese, Korean and some Southeast Asian societies to industrial techniques and disciplines, it also implanted what political scientist James Scott has called a 'high modernist ideology' in many of Japan's former colonies.[22] This would emerge after the war and after independence as a broad consensus belief in the value of technology in mastering nature and fate, the importance of industry for social development and human wellbeing, and the need for rational social order and discipline.

Japan's experience with empire-building ended in defeat and destruction, as well as enduring memories among its neighbours of the savagery of Japanese conquest and occupation. From 1952, Tokyo began to pay reparations to many of its former colonies – and, characteristically, these reparations were different from those paid by other defeated powers. At the core of Japan's reparations was technical assistance in the form of machinery and materials, knowledge and training, and specialist engineers. There was a familiar cast to the sectors targeted – planning, infrastructure, industry, energy and communications – and consequently a marked receptiveness among the societies formerly subject to Tokyo's 'scientific colonialism'. As reparations gave way to development aid, the same logic applied. By 1989, Japan was the world's largest aid donor, providing nearly twice the amount of development assistance as the United States – and its aid predominantly went to regional countries and concentrated on technical assistance.[23]

The motivation was not pure altruism or even just a desire to make amends – there was substantial self-interest in Japan's distinctive reparations and aid payments. Tokyo's technical assistance provided lucrative contracts for Japanese construction firms and industrial conglomerates, nurtured export markets for Japanese manufacturing and eased access to raw materials. There was a distinct pattern of Japanese aid being targeted to sectors and countries in which Japanese business had the greatest interest or saw the most potential. As the economies of South Korea, Taiwan, Hong Kong and Singapore began to register the same sustained rates of high economic growth as Japan, economist Kaname Akamatsu dusted off a forgotten 1930s metaphor to describe how Asia would catch up with the western economies: industrialisation in Asia would resemble a flock of flying geese, whereby successive tiers of countries would follow leading regional economies by adopting their methods, technologies and industries. The key mechanisms would be foreign direct investment by more-developed economies in less-developed economies and technology transfer.[24] The implication was that Asia would follow its own path to rapid industrialisation and development, pioneered in Japan and adopted and adapted by other regional countries. Asia's distinct model would involve the close involvement of the state in economic development, an emphasis on import substitution and export-led growth, controlled exchange rates and a corporatist mobilisation of labour. As the four 'little dragons' – South Korea, Taiwan, Hong Kong and Singapore – had followed Japan, so Thailand, Malaysia, Indonesia and other Asian economies would progress up the path of rapid development.

Tokyo's vision of coordinated development in Asia soon took institutional form. Japanese policymakers were aware that the distinctive characteristics of the Asian development model and Japan's own approach to economic aid did not sit well with the philosophies underpinning the major global institutions: the United Nations, the International Monetary Fund, the Organisation for Economic Co-operation and Development and the World Bank. So they created the Asian Development Bank (ADB) as a genuinely Asia-wide institution, which would protect and promote what they believed was Japan's distinctive approach to development. Again, self-interest was a major motivator as, in its early years, the vast bulk of ADB funding flowed to countries and sectors with which Japan had substantial investment relationships. From the beginning, Japan dominated the

ADB, as its largest funder and source of successive presidents and the largest number of its institutional staff. Within the ADB Japan waged some of its most trenchant battles against a United States that was increasingly critical of what it saw as Asia's statist approach to development. Eventually, under American pressure, the ADB funding began to flow to countries and projects of less immediate interest to Japan's economy. But the bank maintained its strong emphasis on funding the infrastructure and providing access to the technologies that countries needed for industrialisation. The recipient countries eagerly endorsed this approach, and soon imported it into other regional institutions such as ASEAN and the Asia–Pacific Economic Cooperation (APEC) forum.[25]

East Asia's singular history of transnational industrial development goes a long way to explaining this region's role at the cutting edge of a recent transformation in the world economy – global production-sharing. Global production-sharing is the accelerating trend of producing the component parts of elaborate manufactures – cars, phones, computers, cameras, machine tools, pharmaceuticals – in different countries and by different companies as a prelude to their final assembly and export to consumer markets. This trend is transformative in two ways. First, it reverses a two-centuries-long trend in the world economy that had seen larger and larger industrial firms complete more and more of a given production process within their own structures. In economists' jargon, the trend is now towards vertical *dis*-integration, as the global manufacturing giants subcontract increasing segments of their manufacturing chains to outside companies, often located in diverse countries. The second transformation is even more important. Global production-sharing allows companies and countries that, in the past, could never have competed in the brutal world of global manufacturing to industrialise and prosper. By specialising in particular segments of manufacturing, small companies and developing countries find it much easier to access investment and technology, and bind themselves into the global manufacturing sector. And so developing countries' share of the global trade in component parts has increased from a quarter in the early 1990s to one half today.

While production-sharing is a global trend, East Asia is indisputably the world's leading exponent of it. In the past two decades, between 70 and 80 per cent of the growth in manufacturing in East and Southeast Asia has come from global production-sharing. Just eleven economies in East Asia – Japan, South Korea, China, Taiwan, Hong Kong, Vietnam, Thailand, the Philippines, Malaysia, Singapore and Indonesia – export 39 per cent of the world's component parts. And components comprise a much higher proportion of East Asia's internal trade (35 per cent) compared to the global average of 22 per cent. Within Southeast Asia, this trend is even more marked: almost half (44 per cent) of its intra-regional manufacturing trade is made up of component parts.[26]

Economist Prema-chandra Athukorala lists five reasons for East Asia's disproportionate lead in global production-sharing: the region's higher labour productivity-to-cost ratio relative to other regions, more-liberal trade and investment policy settings, high-quality logistics and infrastructure, a long history of welcoming foreign industrial investment, long-term regional stability and proximity to China as both a final assembly hub and a prospective market for finished manufactures.[27] A common denominator, much harder to quantify, underpins these conditions: a 100-year history of transnational development. Nothing has so constantly nagged at the region's sovereignty obsession, ideological rivalries and subregional parochialisms as the constant evidence that Asian economies prosper most under conditions of transnational collaboration and joint development. And according to some economists, the potential for these forms of transnational production-sharing to encompass other parts of Asia – particularly South Asia – is high.

The alacrity with which Asian countries have assisted and encouraged industrial firms to distribute their production processes among Asian economies has undoubtedly been to the collective benefit of all. Major global corporations are drawn to siting their industry in Asia because of host countries' friendliness to foreign investment and their willingness to ensure the seamless flows of component parts to higher and higher stages of the production chain. But with collective prosperity also comes collective vulnerability. Extensive production-sharing among Asian economies makes the manufacturing sector in East and Southeast Asia highly sensitive to disruptions to the supply chain in other countries. When a devastating tsunami hit Fukushima in Japan in March 2011, it cut Japanese automobile production by 47.7 per cent and electrical component production by 8.25 per cent. But Japan's was not the only industrial sector damaged by the Fukushima disaster. The sudden cessation in automobile component exports from Japan also caused a 19.7 per cent drop in Thai auto manufacturing, a 24 per cent drop in that of the Philippines and a 6 per cent drop in that of Indonesia. The interruption of the flow of electrical components out of Japan reduced the volume of exports from the electrical sectors of the Philippines by 17.5 per cent and Malaysia by 8.4 per cent.[28] As they continue to industrialise, Asia's economies have real stakes in each other's fortunes – for better and worse.

Energy Arteries

If manufacturing has drawn together the countries of Asia's eastern coastline, another powerful consequence of development has begun to link them to Asia's other subregions: South, Central and West Asia. As Asia's societies have developed and urbanised, their demand for energy – particularly oil and gas – has increased markedly. Developing countries in Asia have been responsible for over half of the growth in global energy demand since 1990. The International Energy Agency estimates that these countries will account for 63 per cent of the growth in global energy demand to 2035, with China accounting for 31 per cent, India 18 per cent and Southeast Asia 11 per cent. Today, India and China account for one-quarter of world energy consumption, and the consumption of the two Asian giants is predicted to rise to one-third by 2040.[29]

Asia's most rapidly developing societies can't supply their own energy needs now, and will increasingly depend on energy imports into the future. Five of the largest oil importers in the world are Asian. China's energy demand is so great that, even though it has the largest oil reserves in Pacific Asia, it currently imports over half the oil it consumes, with this projected to rise to three-quarters of its oil consumption by 2035. Japan, Taiwan, South Korea and India have few oil reserves of their own, with the first three being almost completely dependent on imports and India over 70 per cent dependent.[30]

Because energy is a bulky commodity that is consumed in large quantities, countries tend to buy it from the closest point of production. For the countries of South, Southeast and Northeast Asia, the closest source of oil and gas is Central and West Asia. Whereas, in 1990, one-third of developing Asia's oil came from the Persian Gulf, today one-half does. And given the projected increase in Asia's energy demands, it is only the vast reserves in West Asia – estimated to hold over half of all the world's proven conventional and unconventional oil reserves – that can slake the Asian giants' thirst for oil and gas.[31] Today, China sources 51 per cent of its oil imports from the Gulf; in 20 years it will be three-quarters. Japan sources 83 per cent of its oil from West Asia, India 64 per cent and South Korea 85 per cent – all these amounts are projected to rise.

Looming large as a single source of energy for Asia's giants is the Kingdom of Saudi Arabia. Riyadh exports three times more oil to its five largest Asian customers – China, India, Japan, South Korea and Singapore – than to Europe and North America combined. Almost half of all Saudi oil production is bound for Asia's big four: China, India, Japan and South Korea. The Saudi Arabian Oil Company, or Saudi Aramco, is the single largest supplier of oil to China, Japan, India, South Korea, Taiwan, Singapore and the Philippines.[32]

For Asia's booming economies, these energy linkages with West Asia are increasingly strategic – if, by strategic, we mean a matter of life and death, today and into the future. Developed or developing economies that no longer have access to dependable long-term supplies of energy at stable prices are at risk of social chaos and political implosion. Energy is the lifeblood not only of burgeoning manufacturing and services sectors but is also crucial to the very capacity of Asian societies to supply their teeming cities with food and water, sanitation and basic transport infrastructure. Electricity and petroleum are the enablers of an expanding middle class on which the political legitimacy of many regimes in Asia depend. And so the oil and gas producers of West Asia are the best guarantors of energy-supply security for developed and developing economies in South, Southeast and Northeast Asia. With almost one-fifth of the world's proven oil reserves, Saudi Arabia has traditionally played the role of the 'swing producer' in the global energy markets, by expanding or reducing its production to smooth out fluctuations in supply and price. Saudi Arabia and the other two Gulf oil giants, Iran and Iraq, represent the most dependable sources of supply as Asia doubles its oil and gas consumption over the next two decades. Of course, all three Gulf oil giants live in an unstable neighbourhood. The prospect of increasingly powerful Asian giants, as they become more deeply dependent on Gulf oil supplies, offering to guarantee the stability and security of their suppliers is increasingly likely.

For the Gulf oil producers – and Saudi Arabia in particular – the energy relationship with Asia's rising powers is equally strategic. Oil production comprises 55 per cent of the Saudi economy and 75 per cent of government revenue. As one of the most authoritarian regimes in the world, overseeing a fast-growing population of which almost half are under the age of twenty-four and 90 per cent are under fifty, Riyadh has traditionally used transfer payments largely funded out of oil revenue to maintain social peace while avoiding political reform.[33] In early 2011, shaken by the 'Arab Spring' revolts in neighbouring countries, the Saudi monarchy announced US$100 billion extra in social benefits payments, particularly in public housing, as well as 60,000 additional jobs in the state security services. Oil revenue is equally crucial to the Kingdom's external security. As a relatively small population sitting atop vast energy wealth, Saudi Arabia feels threatened by the Gulf's two Shiah-majority powers, Iran and Iraq, and has spent billions over successive decades on its military and in bolstering Sunni regimes and causes in West and Central Asia. For Riyadh, a sudden reduction in external demand for oil and gas would be catastrophic. This is why the constant rhetoric, dating from the 1970s oil shocks, from Saudi Arabia's traditional customers in Europe, North America and Japan about the need to reduce their dependence on Middle East energy has been so unsettling. And this is why the emergence of Asia's rapidly expanding energy thirst during the last two decades has been so reassuring – particularly since the discovery of shale oil in the United States has made Saudi Arabia's previous biggest customer a net energy exporter for the first time in half a century.

The links across Asia go beyond the production, transport and consumption of oil. China, Japan and South Korea have all invested in energy assets in the Gulf region, with Asian investors playing a vital role in Saudi Arabia's efforts to diversify its economy by expanding its petrochemicals sector. China is now the largest market for exported Saudi petrochemicals. Saudi Arabia has reciprocated by investing heavily in petroleum-processing plants in China. Meanwhile, the trade between China and Saudi Arabia has increased by a factor of fifty since 1990, with Chinese manufactures rapidly displacing western products in the Saudi market. An International Energy Agency study calculated that two-thirds of every dollar China spends on oil imports from the Organization of the Petroleum Exporting Countries (OPEC) returns to the Chinese economy through purchases of Chinese manufactures. Little wonder that references to 'Asia's new silk road' appear regularly in the public statements of Saudi and Chinese officials as they talk of the economic and strategic links between eastern and western Asia.[34]

Sinews of Concrete and Steel

Other, more tentative, signs of Asia's reintegration shouldn't be discounted either. Subregional organisations have found that adhering to strict demarcations in their membership makes less and less sense. From the mid-1990s, ASEAN has gradually expanded its regular heads-of-state summits, first to include Japan, China and South Korea and then to bring in India, Australia, New Zealand, Russia and the United States. APEC, an organisation that once held rigidly to its Pacific Rim self-definition, now is increasingly tempted to admit India, with its booming economy. The Shanghai Cooperation Organisation, conceived as a forum for states with Central Asian interests, has accepted Afghanistan, Pakistan, India, Mongolia and Iran as observers, and Sri Lanka, Belarus and Turkey as dialogue partners. Given the increasingly strategic economic relationships developing between East, West and South Asia, we may soon see these organisations expanding further or new pan-Asian institutions being born.

More tangible infrastructure is starting to spread across the Asian continent also, reflecting shared beliefs that it is here that the fortunes of Asia's rising economies will be secured. One estimate puts Asia's infrastructure spending at 60 per cent of the global total by 2025.[35] Roads, railways and pipelines are crossing borders and defying Asia's uncompromising geography to give industries access to new markets and trade routes, or to bring the oxygen of commerce to isolated and underdeveloped provinces. A range of subregional infrastructure initiatives, from Central and South Asia to the Mekong subregion, have begun to be connected with each other through large pan-Asian blueprints. Dating from 1992, the Asian Land Transport Infrastructure Development initiative envisages an integrated network of 141,000 kilometres of standardised highways, crossing 155 borders across thirty-two countries in Asia. A more recent vision is that of an energy system linking oil, gas and electricity production, transport and consumption across Asia. A recent study by the Asian Development Bank estimated that if Asia is able to invest US$290 billion in trans-Asian infrastructure between 2010 and 2020, it could lift the income of developing Asia by as much as US$13 trillion.[36]

Asia's emerging infrastructure superpower, China, seems to have been inspired by these visions to develop its own strategic plans. Long accustomed to meeting its own continental-scale infrastructure needs, China has been reaching across geographic barriers to connect with its neighbours for over half a century. There is no greater symbol of the vaulting ambition of China's infrastructure plans than the 1300-kilometre Karakoram Highway, the highest paved road in the world, which spans the ramparts of the Himalayas between Kashgar in China's Xinjiang province and Abbottabad in Pakistan. More recently, China's president, Xi Jinping, has unveiled a major 'strategic conception' of networks of Chinese commerce, investment and infrastructure linking China with the other economies of Asia and beyond. Dubbed 'One Belt, One Road', Xi envisages a 'New Silk Road Economic Belt' stretching from western China across Central Asia and into Europe, and a 'Twenty-First Century

Maritime Silk Road', stretching from the Chinese coast through Southeast Asia and across the Indian Ocean.[37] Responding to the shortfall in investment for Asia's infrastructure needs, Beijing has also launched a multilateral Asian Infrastructure Investment Bank, with twenty-six founding members, to provide over US$50 billion in infrastructure funding to Asian projects.

Much of the boost to infrastructure building across Asia has been driven by rivalry. Japan has responded vigorously to China's emergence as a major transnational investor, announcing major funding initiatives for infrastructure across Southeast Asia. In Central Asia, the competition among Asian powers – China, Japan, Russia and perhaps Iran and India – for access to the region's energy via competing pipelines has been dubbed the 'new great game' for strategic influence in the region.[38] Worried that China's Maritime Silk Road is actually a ploy to build naval dominance in the Indian Ocean, India has countered with a range of initiatives to link Central Asian economies with the Indian Ocean using road and pipeline corridors through Iran, Afghanistan and Pakistan.

Connections across Asian societies are occurring at the human level as well. One more consequence of rapid economic development in Asia is the emergence of a very big consuming and spending middle class. Today, there are half a billion middle-class people in Asia, a number that is projected to triple within the decade. The OECD predicts that, by 2030, Asia will be home to two-thirds of the planet's middle class and be responsible for over 40 per cent of global consumption.[39] As the brilliant American economist Thorstein Veblen observed so acutely over a century ago, the distinguishing feature of the middle class is conspicuous consumption: the acquisition and display of goods and services that advertise one's social position.[40] This is as true in Asia today as it has been in Europe and America historically, and one prominent feature of Asia's conspicuous consumption has been leisure travel. For the past two decades,

Asia's fastest developing economies have become the source of the most dynamic growth in global tourism. According to the World Tourism Association, emerging Asia's rates of international tourist departures have been growing at over 10 per cent per year. What is striking is that Asian tourists are overwhelmingly choosing destinations in other Asian countries for their holidays. Eight of the top-ten international destinations for Chinese tourists are in Asia; for Japanese tourists, Asian countries comprise seven of the top-ten tourism destinations; Indians choose six Asian countries among their top tourism preferences.[41]

For centuries, Asia was a continent defined more by its domination by others and its differences than by any collective identity or essence. At the beginning of the twentieth century, when nationalist writers began to visit each other and talk about pan-Asian values and solidarity, they had to speak to each other in the language of colonisers. Today, while the language barriers remain, the connections among Asian societies are beginning to be more significant than the divisions and differences. Developing Asian economies, once so single-mindedly focused on access to markets in, and investment from, Europe and America, are today very aware that their own economic viability depends increasingly on the dynamic economies of other Asian countries.

One consequence of the increasing connections among Asian societies is that the old habit of subdividing Asia makes less sense with each passing year. Western countries have a tendency to define 'Asia' as including those countries that are believed to be significant at a particular point in time and excluding all other countries occupying the continent. For a long time, Asia was defined by economic success – particularly of the economies of Pacific Asia – while the remainder of the continent, west of the Malay Peninsula, was defined out of the picture. This changed as the Indian economy started to boom: 'Indo-Pacific' Asia replaced 'Asia Pacific' Asia – but again to the exclusion of the rest of the continent.

Persisting with this habit means we are more and more likely to misunderstand what is happening on the earth's largest and most populous continent. As Asian societies' successes and anxieties are increasingly affected by other countries on the continent, developing a clear understanding of Asia means recognising these connections in their entirety – and defining Asia in its entirety: from the Pacific to the Mediterranean, and the Arctic to the Indian Ocean.

3

COMPULSIVE AMBITION

In July 1601, a major riot broke out in the city of Suzhou, the boom town of late Ming Dynasty China. By the beginning of the seventeenth century, Suzhou had become the capital of China's silk industry and a major financial centre, with a population of over half a million people – a global mega-city by the standards of the time. Suzhou's rise had been built on the unceasing demand in Europe, Japan and the Americas for Chinese silks, porcelains and cottons, and their willingness to pay for these goods with galleons full of silver bullion. Silver was the commodity that drew Ming China inexorably into the emerging global economy.[1] The digging of new mines in the mountains of Saxony, Bohemia, Hungary and the Tyrol in the 1450s had reawakened Europe's desire for the luxuries and spices of the Orient, and with the discoveries of massive silver seams in Spanish America and the invention of new refining processes using mercury, Europeans had something the Chinese wanted, which they could trade for the riches of Cathay.

Ming China's insatiable thirst for precious metals had its roots in the decision of the first Ming emperor to institute a paper currency throughout his empire. The value of this new currency soon collapsed because it was not convertible to precious metals, copper coins or silk. Despite the emperor's ban on mining or importing precious metals, silver rapidly became the de facto currency. Eventually, in 1436, the Ming court acquiesced – ultimately demanding payment of all taxes in silver – but the failure of its paper currency had left the legacy of a chronic silver shortage in China.[2]

Silver money and a rising international demand for silks and porcelains transformed imperial Chinese society. The hitherto agrarian economy specialised and commercialised; the silk, cotton and porcelain industries boomed; people streamed into industrial and financial centres such as Suzhou; and a market economy emerged, driven by an expanding and increasingly powerful merchant class and burgeoning regional trade. The flow of silver into China encouraged business speculation and price inflation, but failed to staunch the shortage of precious metals in that rapidly expanding market economy.[3] By the time of the great Suzhou riot in 1601, the Ming economy had come to rely heavily on large imports of silver from Peru, Mexico and Japan to increase the money supply at a rate that would maintain business and consumer confidence.

The riot began when a silk weaver named Ge Xian led a protest, symbolised by a palm-leaf fan, against new taxes levied on silk artisans and dealers. He was particularly enraged by the leading imperial official in Suzhou, Sun Long, a local representative of the corrupt eunuch class that had gained control of the imperial court in Beijing. Ge Xian and the other rioters were careful to exempt merchants and their families from the violence but they beat to death every official and tax collector they could find. After three days of mayhem, Sun Long fled Suzhou and most of the remaining officials were dead. As order returned to Suzhou, Ge Xian was arrested and sentenced to death but perhaps in recognition that there had been some justification to the rioters' anger, the sentence was not carried out. He lived to a ripe old age.[4]

By the time Ge Xian died, the tensions that had led him to pick up the palm-leaf fan of protest had become chronic throughout China. The diarist Song Yingxing, a minor Ming official, could not help but despair at the rising corruption and anarchy of Chinese society.

> For the state, the conflagration set by the eunuchs blazed out of control; for the merchants, misfortunes were brought by spendthrift sons; in various localities profit-seeking bullies assembled; officials became increasingly corrupt; and clerks and runners devised new, wicked techniques. All of these problems grew worse each day. Just as the merchants were about to maneuver their way out of their straits, the new tax levy order fell down upon them and they were afflicted by bandit invasions.[5]

Song's account tells the story of the growing crisis of the Ming Dynasty at ground level, but he was probably unaware of the deeper roots of the crisis in the sudden global shortage of silver. The seemingly endless river of bullion across the Pacific slowed to a trickle in the 1620s as production slumped at the Potosí mine in Upper Peru (now Bolivia) and the Mexican silver mines were hit by chronic mercury shortages. To make matters worse, Dutch and English raiders had started to take a toll on the silver galleons, and Philip IV of Spain decided to crack down on the smuggling of New World silver across the Pacific. The Tokugawa expulsion of Portuguese merchants and prohibition of foreign trade in the 1630s ended Japanese bullion exports. Growing instability in China led to widespread hoarding of silver, while government taxes – in silver – rose in the course of a desperate struggle against invaders from Manchuria. The powerful merchant class, alienated by Ming taxes and restrictions, began to switch its allegiance to the Manchus. The price of silk, cotton and porcelain plummeted, while the price of grains rose by over 200 per cent. Starvation, rioting and banditry became widespread.[6] By the time Manchu forces captured Beijing in April 1644, they found the imperial treasury empty.

The founder of the Ming Dynasty, the Hongwu emperor (who reigned from 1368 to 1398), would have attributed the downfall of his dynasty to his successors' folly in allowing the influence of foreign bullion to distort and disrupt the harmony of Chinese society. A deeply religious man, the Hongwu emperor came to power determined to purify Chinese society from the foreign influences that the Mongol Yuan Dynasty had allowed, to bring it back into harmony with the cosmic order. In 1397 he initiated the Great Ming Code, a constitution designed to reassert traditional values, eradicate foreign influences and extend the virtues of Chinese civilisation to outer barbarians.[7] His issue of inconvertible paper money was designed to cut the Chinese economy off from corrupting foreign trade. From 1371, the Ming Empire had prohibited travel abroad or contact with foreigners on pain of death; ports were blocked and the construction of ships outlawed; foreign goods were to be destroyed. Only foreigners who acknowledged the virtue of Chinese civilisation by paying tribute were granted access to China's market and products – and even then the Hongwu emperor made clear his distaste for foreign trade:

> Foreign merchants ... are attracted by our morality and righteousness, not by profit. How shameful of us to make profit out of them. Even if we do levy duty on them, how little will that be? We lose more dignity than profit![8]

Haijin – the urge to shut out the world for fear that it would disrupt the harmony and integrity of society – was a constant factor in Chinese history after 1371. Periodic liberalisation of contact was soon followed by reimposition of controls. Strict prohibition of contact with foreigners and regulation of foreign trade inevitably provoked piracy, smuggling and corruption at the Empire's borders, only deepening Beijing's prejudices against the defiling influence of the outside world. The Ming Xuande emperor cracked down even harder on outside contact in 1433, despite having authorised the fabulous Indian Ocean expeditions of his eunuch admiral Zheng He. Official records of Zheng's voyages were destroyed. With the opening of the Grand Canal between Beijing and Hangzhou in 1411, the Chinese economy was made independent of ocean trade between the northern and southern empire. The Qing Dynasty, which followed the Ming, reinstated *haijin* in 1647 after the Ming Dynasty had lifted it in 1567. By Qing regulations, all settlements within 30–50 *li* (15–20 kilometres) of the coast had to be evacuated and all boats were to be burned. Later the Qing began to allow closely regulated and taxed foreign trade through a small number of trading ports.[9]

China was not alone in shutting itself off from the corrupting influence of the outside world. With his crushing victory in the Battle of Sekigahara in 1600, Shogun Tokugawa Ieyasu instituted a strictly hierarchic *bakuhan* system of control over provincial *daimyos* in Japan. Japan's era of *tenka taihei* (the great peace) under the Tokugawa shogunate relied on keeping Japanese society inwardly focused and tightly regulated. Fearing the influence of Christian missionaries and the enrichment of provincial *daimyos* through foreign trade, in 1633 the shogun announced the policy of *sakoku*, prohibiting all travel abroad by Japanese, restricting all foreigners to the port of Nagasaki and banning foreigners from learning the Japanese language. *Sakoku* was designed also to withdraw Japan from the Chinese tributary system and to build the sophistication and prestige of Japan's own social and cultural system.[10] By the nineteenth century, *sakoku* had developed into an ideology of seclusion and superiority among Japan's elites.

Korea's Choson Dynasty took seclusion from outside influences even further than the Chinese and Japanese. Following devastating invasions by the Japanese and Manchus in the seventeenth century, the Choson emperors forbade any travel abroad by Koreans, the building of ocean-going boats or any contact with foreigners.[11] Contact with Japanese traders was limited to the island of Tsushima, and the few Chinese embassies that visited were confined to a walled compound and allowed no contact with Koreans. An intensely negative attitude to foreigners accompanied *silhak*, a period of intense innovation and development of Korean culture.

For all three societies, seclusion ended at the barrel of a cannon. The Qing Dynasty's attempts to control the inflow of opium and the outflow of silver provoked a violent response from the British in 1840. Thereafter, China was forcibly opened to merchants, missionaries and mercenaries, triggering rising chaos in the decaying Qing empire. An explicit threat of the same fate accompanied Commodore Matthew Perry's black ships into Tokyo Bay in July 1853, sparking a revolution in Japanese society based on an intense hunger to learn the secret of western power. Korea's turn came in 1871 when an American marine expedition against Ganghwa Island killed 243 Koreans; soon after the Choson emperor opened trade relations with the United States and Japan.

For Asia's societies, the age of imperialism brought globalisation at gunpoint. Asian economies were reshaped by the rhythms and appetites of Europe's industrial revolution: whatever Europe's factories and middle classes wanted came to determine what Asian economies produced, but anything that competed with what Europe exported soon withered. Expansion and contraction in Asian economies followed the business cycles of Europe and America, and as they became appendages of their colonisers, Asian societies' economic fragility increased. Periodic famines killed millions and poverty rose steadily. For many Asian countries, the period of economic domination also brought sustained social and political upheaval.

It was little wonder that governments that came to power after independence or revolution closed their economies to the global market and relied heavily on the state to build unity and development and forestall social unrest. In each, the formula was slightly different, but the broad outlines were remarkably similar across very different societies. In state after state – whether communist, authoritarian or democratic – single-party governments held power for long decades. The governing party became the symbol of independence; of national ideals, unity and identity; of justice and redress; of pride, defence and development – in the case of the Congress Party in India, the Liberal Democratic Party in Japan, China's and Vietnam's communist parties, military regimes in Pakistan and Korea, Malaysia's United Malays National Organisation, Singapore's People's Action Party and Taiwan's Kuomintang. At the slightest sign of social unrest – whether urban activism, ethnic rivalry or rural revolt – the dominant party tightened its control.[12]

Asia's states each assumed a central role in guiding and developing the economy also. The full powers of the state were bent towards building self-sufficiency and fostering the development of local industry. In some of Asia's states, such as Japan, Taiwan, Korea and Singapore, the state played a technocratic role. Economic bureaucrats were carefully selected and trained and given great latitude to play a decisive role in development through powerful planning agencies. They set targets in terms of growth and competitiveness, closely regulated the financial system to maximise investment, and exercised influence through institutionalised elite networks. In other countries, such as Indonesia, Malaysia and Burma, state involvement was patronage-based. More informal networks connected entrenched elites with government institutions to channel the benefits of rapid development towards favoured groups. In each case, governments explicitly linked legitimacy with the capacity to deliver economic growth, improve living standards and maintain social stability.

With very few exceptions, Asian governments vigorously protected their domestic markets from external influence. Through a mixture of high tariffs, strict import quotas and outright import bans, Asian states sought to eliminate the impact of western multinational firms on their domestic markets while boosting the development of their own industries. Running through all of these policies was a potent suspicion of unrestrained capitalism and a determination to seek other means of economic development. Communist China opted for Soviet-style planning which nationalised and collectivised every aspect of the economy. Rapid economic development would be delivered through an act of the collective will as the party mobilised the people in a series of mass campaigns targeting high growth targets. Non-communist India tried to steer a path that was neither capitalist nor communist, marrying Gandhian communal action with Jawaharlal Nehru's preferences for socialist industrial transformation. Some institutions were nationalised while others were subjected to close state regulation, and centralised five-year plans set the economic agenda. In the Asian 'tiger' economies, starting with Japan, governments sought economic growth through boosting exports into open western markets while strictly controlling investment and trade access into their own domestic economies. Whatever their development strategy, most Asian governments instituted strong capital and exchange controls as another line of defence against the global economy.

But through the 1970s and 1980s, as developed economies entered a protracted period of instability and low growth, Asia's economies began to open up. The reasons were varied – the need to access resources, energy and technology; threats of trade retaliation from the western markets they so relied on; a growing interest in the integrity of the global trading system – but the results were remarkably parallel. The Asian state was retreating from its prominent role in directing and managing the economy, dominating the private sector and boosting the public sector, in favour of a more facilitative and regulatory role. The sharpest departure came in China, where Deng Xiaoping and his supporters ditched Mao's focus on production relations and heavy industry in favour of productivity and efficiency and boosting consumption. Key to Deng's plans was opening the Chinese economy to the outside world, through special economic zones, encouragement of investment and technology imports and emulation of the Asian tigers' export-oriented growth strategies. India's liberalisation followed a severe balance-of-payments crisis in 1991, dismantling stifling controls on industry, imports and foreign exchange, and more gradually removing capital controls.[13] Eventually, the momentum behind opening up Asia's economies gave rise to a distinctive form of regionalism through APEC, in which each member economy unilaterally pledged to dismantle its barriers to trade and investment. Asia's successful economies had become part of an increasingly open global economy, and the international economy had become an essential part of their own success and dynamism.

The Growth Treadmill

From the outside, the success of Asia's boom economies is stunning. The doubling of per capita income, a feat that took Britain half a century and America three decades, was achieved in under ten years by Japan, the Republic of Korea, Singapore, China and India. In the thirty years after Deng's liberalising reforms, the Chinese economy grew by a factor of fourteen to become the second largest in the world, and China became the largest holder of foreign reserves and the world's largest trading nation. In the two decades following its market reforms, India's economy quadrupled in size and entered the world's top-ten largest economies. Just ten years after the Asian financial meltdown, Indonesia's economy had doubled in size from its pre-crisis high. From the perspective of Asia's citizens, too, there is much to applaud about the rise of Asian economies. Across Asia, over one million people progressed out of the World Bank's poverty range each week during the decades leading to and following the turn of the millennium. Consumer items that were unknown or tantalisingly rare in the era of self-sufficiency became widespread: televisions, computers, mobile phones, refrigerators, cars. Ways of life that had seemed impossibly distant became increasingly within reach with each passing year.

But for governments, the reality of rapid economic growth has been much less glamorous. 'Development' – a benign, optimistic term easily bandied about by economists and activists – unleashes powerful forces that reshape a society, paying little heed to the wishes of rulers, elected or not. For governments that had for decades seen themselves as the shapers and enablers of their own societies, the process of development has been by turns baffling, exhilarating, confounding and terrifying. No country that has undergone industrialisation and modernisation has escaped profound churn in its society, economy and politics, but those that developed earlier seem to have been more lightly affected. For countries of the scale of Asia's rising powers, experiencing the fastest rates of economic development in human history, the social, political and cultural consequences of growth have been very unsettling.

The first troubling symptom was urbanisation. Societies that had been predominantly rural and agriculture-based started to experience the unregulated flow of millions of people into cities. As it started in England 350 years ago, so it continues today in Asia, where India and China are experiencing the fastest rates of urban growth in history. Since 1978, over half a billion Chinese have flowed into China's cities; a country that was less than one-fifth urban in 1978 is now over one-half urban. China's urbanisation rate is five times its population growth rate – and the process of urbanisation is accelerating. In the last decade alone, over 100 million people have moved to the teeming cities. In the forty years to 2010, one-quarter of a billion people moved to India's cities; it is estimated that the next quarter-billion increment will take half as long.[14] India's and China's Asian neighbours have experienced similarly high rates of urbanisation. Over the thirty years of its most intensive industrialisation, the Republic of Korea's urban population increased by 45 per cent (1960–1990), Japan's by 40 per cent (1950–1980), Malaysia's by 30 per cent (1970–2000) and Indonesia's by 28 per cent (1970–2000).[15] By contrast, during the three decades of its most intensive industrialisation, Britain's urban population grew by 17 per cent (1850–1880) and America's by 18 per cent (1880–1910).

There is no great mystery behind this largest movement of humans in history. The urban–rural wealth disparity widens rapidly during the process of economic development. Between 2000 and 2010, the average income of a resident of Shenzhen in China climbed from RMB 35,000 to 82,000 and for the average Shanghainese from RMB32,000 to 66,000. In comparison, the average rural income was RMB7900 in 2010. China's cities of over 2.5 million people have been estimated to generate 95 per cent of its wealth.[16] Cities promise not only money, but also opportunity. One recent study estimates that 70 per cent of all new employment in the Indian economy will occur in the cities over the next 30 years.[17] Of course, urban–rural disparities even out over time. Economic history shows that as people leave the land, agriculture becomes more productive. Unburdened by millions of underemployed people living semi-subsistence lifestyles, the agricultural economy is freed to make use of larger units of cultivation and to invest profits from selling produce on the open market in seeds, livestock, fertilisers and machinery. Over time, developed countries have found that the initial widening disparities in urban–rural income have narrowed and vanished as the rural sector becomes more productive.

But that prospect seems a long way away to societies in the early stages of rapid economic development. The reality of millions of their citizens each year autonomously deciding to leave traditional self-sufficient rural communities and move to cities is deeply unsettling to governments. Indonesia's cities are growing by 4.2 per cent each year, the Philippines' by 3.4 per cent and Vietnam's by 3.1 per cent. The pattern is clear in country after country: it is the largest cities that are growing fastest. People seeking a better future crowd into slums and packed tenements; the World Bank estimates that between one-third and one-fifth of the urban population of developing countries live in slums. New Delhi's population has grown from 1.4 million to 15.6 million since 1950 and, over that time, its identifiable slum clusters have mushroomed from 200 to 1160. No government on earth has been able to cope with the uncontrolled growth of its cities during industrialisation. Problems of crime, pollution, public order and disease grow and spread. Infrastructure building by definition is inadequate, but, with a perverse logic, those cities that are more effective at building infrastructure are penalised with even higher rates of population growth.

Recently, the World Bank surveyed the attitudes of developing-country governments to the process of urbanisation that their countries were undergoing: three-quarters of respondents saw urbanisation as dangerous and wished to slow or reverse the process.[18] China has actively sought to stem and redirect the flow of urbanisation. In the late 1970s, it instituted the *hukou* system of household registration with the intention of making the decision of citizens to move to the cities dependent on the approval of the government. Those living in cities without the authorising *hukou* would be denied access to services and social security.[19] The system has not worked. Today there are an estimated quarter of a billion

Chinese living in cities without *hukou* or access to services. The system is being scrapped. Another stratagem tried by the Chinese government is to build new second- and third-tier cities to absorb rural migration. Again, the policy has not worked. In the five years to 2005, Beijing's population increased by 6.6 per cent per year and Shanghai's by 9.1 per cent.[20]

The next worrying trend of development is a pronounced change in the structure of the economy. Developing economies become less agricultural and more heavily invested in manufacturing and services. In 1978, 70 per cent of China's labour force worked in agriculture, 17 per cent in manufacturing and 12 per cent in services; by 2007 just 28 per cent of Chinese workers were agricultural, while 26 per cent were industrial and 32 per cent worked in the service sector. Over the same period, India's agricultural workforce fell from 71 to 51 per cent, while its manufacturing workforce increased from 13 to 18 per cent and its service sector workforce jumped from 16 to 25 per cent. Indonesia's trends have been similar across the same period: agricultural employment has dropped from 61 to 46 per cent, while manufacturing has expanded from 8 to 12 per cent and services from 24 to 42 per cent.[21] Unsurprisingly, nearly all of the growth in manufacturing and services employment in Asia's developing societies has occurred in their expanding cities.

What's so worrying about the growth in a country's urban industrial and services workforce? Take a look at history. People working in manufacturing and services no longer produce what they personally need to survive. They become totally reliant on their jobs to obtain enough money to buy food, accommodation and energy. And they come to rely on different forms of food, accommodation and energy than their counterparts back on the farm. Between 1980 and 2010, the average calorie intake of Chinese people increased by nearly 50 per cent to reach similar levels to those of Japan and the Republic of Korea. Over that thirty years, the average protein intake in China doubled and the average fat intake tripled. Similar consumption changes are occurring in other fast-developing Asian economies.[22] As people urbanise, their energy consumption increases rapidly and changes in form. Cities are, on average, three times as energy-intensive as rural dwellings. And whereas traditional agricultural society relies on traditional energy – wood, wind, water and muscle power – urban living relies on modern energy: electricity, petrol and gas. Cities become teeming centres of constant dependence suspended in webs of supply and demand: demand for what they produce, providing residents with money to buy what they need to survive; supply, delivering a constant stream of the necessities of life. People who move to cities have to improve their lot in order to survive; the safety net of subsistence has been permanently cast aside.

History also shows that the rapid accumulation of people into cities and wage labour can be socially and politically disruptive. The escalating rate of social change experienced by developed societies over the past two centuries could not have occurred without the crowding of people into cities. Urbanisation removes people from the traditional structures of meaning and social control that surround them in their rural villages, and places them in the constant stream of opinion, expectation and aspiration that flows through any city. Political demands and ideologies take root and spread. In the cities the roles and shortcomings of governments are most apparent, inequities and corruption are most clearly drawn, and failures in infrastructure and services snowball into causes of public anger.

For governments, the dilemmas of development are constant and escalating. High rates of growth need to be maintained to keep rapidly growing urban populations employed, fed, housed and powered. Economic growth crowds out other social goals. It is at the heart of the political compact in Asia's rising societies: governments unable to provide continuing high growth rates can feel their mandates to govern crumbling. What's more, the demands of further growth seem to progressively strip away any control that governments once had over their own economies. There is no going back to self-sufficiency. The wrenching changes brought to economy and society by each phase of development in turn generate their own challenges, many of which can only be addressed by embracing further change. The efficient operation of each sector of the economy demands the reform and opening up of allied and associated sectors. Development resembles a fish trap – once a society has begun the process it can't back out. Survival depends on moving forward, stripping back government control, wading deeper and deeper into the rhythms and strictures of the hyper-globalising world economy.

The Lure of the Global

It's not long before an industrialising economy butts up against the limitations of its domestic market. Its own consumers are poor and have very basic needs; its systems of research and innovation are shallow; its supply of investment and infrastructure meagre. Once the process of manufacturing, profit and reinvestment has been uncorked, the momentum is unstoppable. The search for profits and scale soon outstrips the demand produced by domestic consumption and accumulation. Beyond the domestic economy's limits lies salvation. The global market can provide the necessary momentum, the depth and scale of demand necessary to build a modern industrial society. The Atlantic economies, in Europe and North America, offer almost one billion cashed-up and willing customers. Only that vast sea of consumption can provide the market niches and specialisations, the profits and bottomless acquisitiveness, the constant churn of shifting tastes and fashions that can challenge and reward the nascent industries and service-providers of Asia.

The outside world also provides the money and technology needed to take an industrialising economy up the development ladder. A modernising economy needs extensive and increasingly sophisticated infrastructure: roads, railways, ports, communications networks, power grids. Making more valuable and elaborate goods while keeping prices down requires specialist knowledge, from research to engineering to management. Economists estimate that from 1978 to the mid-1990s, China's growth was largely internally driven, mainly through accumulation and the growth of internal consumption. Since then, it has been predominantly externally driven, spurred by the growth of its merchandise exports and inward flows of foreign direct investment.[23] Many of the Asian tiger economies wasted little time on domestic consumption, hitching their industrialisation to export markets almost from the start.

At the same time, a rapidly developing society finds itself decreasingly self-sufficient in terms of food, resources and energy. The change in consumption towards high-protein, heavily processed diets quickly outstrips the capacity of the domestic agricultural sector to meet demand. The loss of rural land to cities and lags in agricultural productivity further decrease self-sufficiency. Even with its abundance of land, China is now under 98 per cent self-sufficient in food and 92 per cent self-sufficient in grains.[24] Many Asian states have become exporters of staples such as rice but major importers of other foods as their populations make the transition away from traditional diets.

Energy soon becomes another vector of deepening external dependence. Modern energy, unlike traditional energy, is unevenly spread through the earth's crust. Even industrialising countries with reasonably large energy reserves soon find that demand outstrips supply: such was the case with the United States by 1962 and with China by 1993. The scale of Asia's societies, and the velocity of their growth, has hypercharged their need for energy way beyond the capacity of their reserves. Asian states dominate the rankings of the world's largest oil importers. Even though it has the largest oil reserves in Pacific Asia, China currently imports over half the oil it consumes, with imports projected to rise to three-quarters of its oil consumption by 2035. Japan, South Korea and India have much smaller indigenous reserves than China and are even more dependent on imports – now and into the future.[25]

Mineral resources are often another widening external dependency. Heavy and light industry demand a range of minerals, while infrastructure needs vast supplies of concrete, steel and other metals. Even countries with sizeable reserves, such as India's iron-ore fields or China's coal beds, often lack the technology and logistics to exploit the reserves more cheaply than they can buy the resources from more-efficient producers overseas. As we have seen, developing Asian economies also heavily depend on the outside world as part of extensive production networks: without the steady supply of component parts or the ability to supply components to other parts of the chain, significant parts of their manufacturing sectors would become moribund.

As an industrialising economy internationalises in search of markets, investment, food, energy and minerals, its financial system comes under pressure to deregulate and internationalise. A closed or highly regulated financial system places important obstacles in the way of rapid development. Industry can be restricted in its access to capital and technology, while domestic investors are hampered in their ability to invest in other countries. Capital controls increase financing costs, reduce the amount of available investment funds and encourage corruption and rent-seeking. Companies buying and selling in the global market with a currency that is not freely convertible to other currencies pay significant costs in money and efficiency to do so. All these factors can have a significantly retarding effect on an emerging economy's growth rate.

The urge for Asia's new developers to join the international economy is not new. The same internationalising imperatives were as irresistible for the first economies to industrialise in Europe and North America. Britain and France, the Netherlands and Belgium, Germany and Italy, the United States and Japan all found their burgeoning industrial economies soon hitting the limits of their domestic markets, causing regular boom-and-bust cycles. These gyrations of economic instability had worrying political implications. With each lurch of the economy, thousands of their citizens joined the ranks of revolutionary movements: Chartists, Jacobins, liberals, socialists, anarchists, communists. The internationalising imperative was therefore doubly acute for the governments and elites of industrialising economies.

The off-the-shelf form of internationalisation for the early industrialisers was imperialism. Colonies and economic satellites promised a cure for most of the agonies of industrialisation: deep and extensive markets providing steady demand for industrial products, capital repatriated through taxation and profits for investment and infrastructure, luxury consumables to satisfy refined domestic tastes, reliable supplies of raw materials at rock-bottom prices, and a resettlement safety valve for booming populations and crowded cities. The first movers' colonies hedged the risks and absorbed the turmoil of their industrialisation. By the time they acceded to their colonies' independence, the colonisers were mature economies and stable advanced societies. Most had well-established stable constitutional and democratic systems of government. Order had been imposed on urbanisation, mainly through extensive infrastructure and services. Their societies became extremely wealthy and well educated, with well-established innovation cultures, economic equality restored, generous social safety nets and high degrees of social cohesion.

The imperial option no longer exists for Asia's late-mover industrialisers. Colonialism has acquired a bad reputation, not least among those who so recently experienced it. As they emerge into the international economy, Asia's economies have found themselves in a phenomenally crowded global marketplace. The world's consumer markets are large and dynamic, but also saturated with consumer goods of astonishing range, quality and sophistication. Global capital markets are deep and liquid, but highly volatile. The scale of global demand for food, energy and minerals has driven their prices higher and made their supply subject to unpredictable fluctuations. The option of owning huge reserves of the energy and minerals an economy needs or the agricultural produce its expanding cities consume is no longer on the table. Decades of exploration and exploitation have sewn up most of the high-yield, low-cost resource real estate on earth. Most production of minerals or energy on the planet is now tightly controlled by state-owned companies or highly restrictive foreign-ownership regulations. What's left is the unconventional, the high risk, the expensive or hard to access. To those new to the process, it seems a very lopsided bargain. A global economy that is so insistent about gaining access to every corner of emerging Asian economies seems implacably unsympathetic to their own internationalising imperatives.

Costs and Claustrophobia

Western societies that anxiously watch the challenge of Asia's industrialising giants will be surprised by these anxieties. China's rise as the world's largest trading state, Taiwan's and Korea's vaulting to the lead in the global technology economy and the astounding success of India's service industries all seem to belie the difficulties of operating in a crowded global marketplace. But what looks to be an inexorable rush to success from the outside looks much less certain from within.

Governments overseeing large, rapidly developing economies are like first-time water-skiers. Tempering the exhilaration of the ride is the fear of the death wobbles, or a basic mistake or an unseen obstacle or current that brings the whole experience to a painful and humiliating end. Development has changed their societies irreversibly, unleashing demands for even greater economic success and improvement. For an urbanising economy rapidly expanding its manufacturing and services sectors, the rapid slowdown of economic growth would leave millions without work and income – and likely to blame the government for their fate. Few Asian governments have forgotten the effects of the Asian financial crisis, when high rates of economic development went into abrupt reverse in 1997 and 1998: the Indonesian economy shrank by 13 per cent, the Thai economy by 10.5 per cent and the Republic of Korea's and Malaysia's by 7 per cent. Indonesia's poverty rate almost doubled to over one-fifth of its population, Korea's more than doubled to almost one-fifth, and Malaysia's and Thailand's climbed well into double figures. In Indonesia the average household income fell by 40 per cent at a time when food prices rose by 81 per cent. Public anger and frustration with the government spilled onto the streets and the spectre of ethnic and communal violence flared for the first time since the 1960s. The long-running, stable rule of the autocratic President Suharto came to an end amid a humiliating International Monetary Fund (IMF) intervention and growing protest movements.[26]

Interruptions to the supply of reasonably priced energy and food can have similarly devastating effects on developing economies and, in turn, destabilise their governments. A decade after the Asian financial crisis, a simultaneous and sustained worldwide increase in energy and food prices caused severe disruption across the developing world. As wheat, milk and meat prices doubled, and rice and soybean prices rose to ten-year highs in the space of months in 2008, serious rioting broke out in scores of developing countries, including Bangladesh, Brazil, Egypt, Indonesia and Yemen. By December 2010, persistently high food prices contributed to the self-immolation of street vendor Mohamed Bouazizi in Tunis, sparking sustained unrest that ultimately toppled the regime of President Zine al-Abidine Ben Ali. The Tunisian protests were taken up across the Arab world, felling dictators in Libya and Egypt and destabilising others in Syria, Iran and Bahrain.

Growth in developing Asia has become not a luxury but a matter of social stability and regime survival. By the mid-1990s, economists estimated that the Chinese economy had to deliver an annual growth rate of at least 7 per cent in order to employ the flow of people entering China's cities and absorb the workers laid off from reforming state-owned corporations.[27] The unspoken 'or else' proposition was the renewed popular protests akin to those leading up to the 1989 Tiananmen massacre, and the Chinese Communist Party's worst nightmare: an unravelling of its rule similar to what happened in the Soviet Union. Even democratic governments are not immune to being dismissed for producing below-par growth rates. In May 2014, the ruling Congress-led coalition in India suffered a landslide defeat in national elections, having been judged harshly for presiding over a sustained sag in India's growth rates to below 5 per cent.

For developing states, the prospect of their growth booms tapering away is not hard to imagine. Asia is dotted with economies that initially grew quickly but settled into sluggish rates of growth long before reaching the developed-country gold standard of stability and comfort. The term for this tendency is the 'middle-income trap' – an economy grows quickly while its wages are comparatively low, but fails to transition to a high-tech economy as its labour costs rise. It becomes wedged between competition from low-wage economies and the continued dominance of high-tech production by developed countries. The Asian Development Bank records that thirty-three of its Asian economies have transitioned to the middle-income stage but just five have broken through to high-income status. Countries such as Malaysia, the Philippines and Thailand have remained in the middle-income range for over fifty years.[28]

The danger of growth slowing too quickly has had a galvanising effect on Asia's rising economies. The Asian economies that transitioned to high-income status – Japan, South Korea, Taiwan, Singapore – all relied on high rates of education and research to do so. Many who want to emulate them have taken up the education challenge, but the problems are complex. Indonesia's rate of tertiary education is so low that it currently produces 40 per cent fewer engineers than its economy needs – and on current trends that shortfall will rise to 70 per cent by 2025.[29] Realising that its rate of enrolment in tertiary education sits at around half the global average, India has set forth an ambitious goal of lifting its enrolment rate to 30 per cent by 2020. But to reach this target, it will need to create 25 million new tertiary education places, or the equivalent of 10,510 technical institutes, 15,530 professional colleges and 521 universities – by 2020.[30] China leads the pack in terms of the energy of its response to the education challenge. Since focusing on education in 1998, it has tripled the proportion of its gross domestic product dedicated to education, doubling the number of tertiary institutions and quintupling the number of tertiary students. Its tertiary education enrolment rate has leapt to 60 per cent of high-school graduates from just 20 per cent in the 1980s. Whereas China's colleges and universities produced 870,000 graduates in 1998, they are currently graduating over 6 million each year.[31]

But China's achievement in boosting education, and India's and Indonesia's aspirations towards the same, is no guarantee of success or stability. The experience of South Korea, where 70 per cent of high school graduates go to university, suggests a worrying scenario. In a country where 43 per cent of the population has a tertiary degree – up from 6 per cent in 1970 – there are simply not enough professional jobs for tertiary graduates. In 2010, just 55 per cent of graduates found professional jobs, down from 74 per cent in 2005. With an estimated excess of 50,000 tertiary graduates to appropriate-level jobs produced every year, the South Korean economy has developed a debilitating skills surplus and problems of underemployment, producing an escalating drag on economic growth and mounting social problems. Already, China is registering similar worrying symptoms. Between 2003 and 2009 the wages of tertiary graduates in China declined in real terms, compared to a nearly 80 per cent rise in manufacturing wages. In the local slang, underemployed tertiary graduates are called the 'ant tribe' because they settle in crowded urban centres and compete for low-paying and unsatisfying jobs.[32]

As they start to rise through middle-income status, developing economies become ever more slaves to the need to produce economic growth. Even those that succeed in educating their growing urban populations must then find the jobs to employ them when they graduate. The desperation of these graduates to find rewarding and appropriate employment – many of them are educated by virtue of their parents emptying their bank accounts to pay for their education and require a well-paying job to acquire the accoutrements of the middle-class lifestyle they aspire to – could quickly flip into frustration and resentment.

Confronted by the daunting scale of their future growth challenge, it is unsurprising that Asia's rising powers are intensely sensitive to any and all perceived obstacles to their success. While rapid economic development in Asia has benefited greatly from relatively open global markets, a ready supply of investment and expertise, stable systems of property rights and risk management, and highly developed logistics and transport infrastructures, there is no abundance of gratitude towards the outside world in Asian societies. For most people who think about international affairs in these societies, the way the world works appears to be very unfair. When they look at today's world, they see an oligopoly: a set of institutions, properties and understandings designed to preserve the privileges of the western elite that originated them. And despite the west's protestations to the contrary, global institutions and settlements seem to be used regularly to advance the interests of developed nations.

One global verity that has come in for major recent criticism is the US dollar, which has overwhelmingly dominated as the global trading currency for more than half a century. In 2009, the governor of the People's Bank of China, Zhou Xiaochuan, publicly criticised the dominance of the greenback, arguing that it delivered enormous privileges to the United States while exporting the instability of the American economy to the rest of the world. Zhou's critique was joined by others as the US Federal Reserve embarked on successive rounds of 'quantitative easing', whose sudden tapering off caused serious problems in several emerging economies.[33] India's top central banker, Raghuran Rajan, and his Indonesian counterpart, Muhamad Chatib Basri, were savage in their criticism of the selfishness and irresponsibility of American monetary policy, given the US dollar's role in broader international finance.[34]

Seen from a developing country's perspective, global institutions also look heavily skewed towards preserving the interests of the privileged minority that live in western countries. Decision-making structures in the UN Security Council, the IMF, the World Bank and the Group of Twenty (G20) seem lopsidedly weighted in favour of America and Western Europe. The English language and western systems of international and public law are slowly gaining universal application. The global economy is dominated by American, European and Japanese companies. The world military balance is overwhelmingly slanted in favour of the United States and its allies.

Western education and popular culture appear to be an implacable, unchallengeable global citadel.

Such perceptions feed intense sensitivity to how rising Asian states' interests are treated outside their borders. People in South Korea still remember the lack of sympathy for their plight of their longstanding ally the United States and the western-dominated IMF during the Asian financial crisis. Many Indians recall the humiliation of the 1991 currency crisis, when its gold-obsessed society had to airlift a significant proportion of its gold reserves to the Bank of England and the IMF before any relief was forthcoming. Some in Japan question their country's long record in providing large slabs of funding to the UN, as Tokyo's longstanding bid for a permanent seat on the Security Council seems as unlikely to be successful as ever. China's business elites concentrate not on their foreign investment successes but on their failures: the rejection of the China National Offshore Oil Company's bid for the Union Oil Company of California in 2005, the Aluminum Corporation of China's failed bid for Rio Tinto in 2009, the American and Australian blocking of Huawei's telecommunications deals on national security grounds. In a 2010 report, China's Ministry of Commerce surveyed all of China's recent failed investment deals and reported that 65 per cent of these were due to unfair foreign regulations.[35]

One effect is to inculcate an outsider mindset towards the institutions and norms of the international system. Asia's rising powers tend to be reticent and self-interested in multilateral settings: willing to go along with the rules when these coincide with their interests, but determined to evade or oppose anything that threatens to impede their progress or impinge on their prerogatives. To those in the west who hope they will become 'responsible stakeholders'[36] in the evolving rules of global affairs, Asia's powers appear frustratingly unwilling to invest in global governance.

The combination of an intense focus on their future growth

challenges and a conviction that the world is weighted against them breeds a distinct form of strategic claustrophobia among several of Asia's powers. It is a pervasive underlying concern that, whether intentionally or not, the way the world works will frustrate their continuing economic growth and rise to power and status. It is a suspicion that the global system built by the age of imperialism, with all the power and wealth disparities that defined it, will be defended at every turn by those it favours.

Another compounding anxiety is that the global economy on which Asia's growing economies are becoming increasingly dependent is more and more unstable. Whereas in the 1970s and 1980s a major economic crisis occurred somewhere in the global economy every three or four years, after the 1990s the frequency of major instability has tightened to every two years.[37] Memories of the Asian financial crisis and the economic, social and political devastation it wrought across the region are still very fresh in Asia – including in countries that largely escaped its worst effects.

Asia's rising powers are caught in a bind. Worry about the internal fragilities that accompany economic development is making them more dependent on an unstable and unsympathetic global economy. They no longer have the option of cutting themselves off from turbulence beyond their borders – they have long passed the threshold of no return. A sudden seclusion would cause the massive disruptions and dislocations they fear most. The only solution is to try to use their growing wealth and power to restructure the world around them in ways that are more conducive to predictability and stability and more compatible with the needs of their own economies. Recently, Chinese president Xi Jinping spoke of the need for China to secure its growth by creating 'a more enabling international environment'.[38]

It is little wonder, then, that the countries of Asia have spent the years since the Asian financial crisis trying to build resilience at home and collective mechanisms among themselves to try to defend against what they see as an unstable and unsympathetic global economic system. In 2010, the countries of Southeast and Northeast Asia launched the Chiang Mai Initiative, a currency-swap arrangement worth US$240 billion to be placed at the disposal of any member country facing a currency crisis. They persisted with the initiative despite the objections of the United States and other western countries that it constituted an alternative to the IMF and thus diluted the IMF's discipline on member economies. In 2014, Brazil, Russia, India, China and South Africa announced the formation of a US$100 billion New Development Bank to provide relief for liquidity pressures in times of crisis and investment for infrastructure in emerging economies. They explicitly tied the formation of this new 'BRICS bank' to frustration with the lack of reform of the Bretton Woods institutions, such as the IMF, and the need to 'rebalance' the global economy from dominance by Europe, America and Japan. More recently, China's announcement of a new multilateral Asian Infrastructure Investment Bank has rightly been seen as a challenge to existing institutions such as the World Bank and the Asian Development Bank. The arrival of new institutions proposed and bankrolled by Asia's claustrophobic rising powers heralds the beginnings of major change to the governance and functioning of the global economy.

Asia's rising powers have found that economic growth brings with it real vulnerabilities. At home it brings worrying social and economic restructuring that seems only resolvable with further development – but this can only be purchased at the price of further integration with an unstable and unsympathetic global economy. The result is strategic claustrophobia, the worry that as the countries rise, space, access and empathy are in increasingly short supply beyond their borders. This breeds an obsessive dissatisfaction; despite having benefited from the existing global economic order,

Asia's rising powers feel little investment in or loyalty to the rules and conventions of that order. People in the west see a ruthlessness and exploitativeness, in business practices, intellectual property, the information commons and international law and security, that appears to them both unjustified and unconscionable. The result is a global economy of increasing interdependence but declining trust, of collective concern about instability but eroding consensus on what to do about it. As Asia's powers continue to rise, so will their sense of claustrophobia; despite their worries about domestic fragility, they will become more obsessively, but selfishly, internationalist.

4

RESTLESS SOULS

When the architect Edwin Lutyens was commissioned to design a new district of the city of Delhi as the seat of government in British India, he chose to align the central vista of what was to become New Delhi with a crumbling red sandstone fort called the Purana Qila. The symbolism of the design was deliberate. Construction of the Purana Qila was begun in the sixteenth century during the reign of the second Mughal emperor Humayun, and finished by his vanquisher, the Afghan king Sher Shah Suri. It was fabled to have been built on the ruins of an older palace, the Indraprastha, the seat of government of the Pandavas, a royal family that features in the Hindu epic the *Mahabharata*. The Purana Qila was known to Lutyens as the oldest standing building in Delhi: its massive 18-metre red sandstone walls and soaring domed turrets were a classic example of early Indo-Persian architecture and referenced in Lutyens's design of the new government buildings; its site recalling the ancient civilisation of India.[1]

The historical and cultural symbolism of Purana Qila was the main reason that Jawaharlal Nehru, the vice-president of the Executive Council of India, decided to hold an Asian Relations Conference in its grounds in March and April 1947. A more prosaic reason was its size: Purana Qila's 1.5-kilometre-long walls would enclose some 200,000 Muslim refugees only months later during India's blood-drenched partition from Pakistan. The fact that India was not yet independent – and nor were most of the Asian nations invited to attend – was partly the point; in a tour of Southeast Asia in March 1946, Nehru had discussed with several independence leaders the need for a conference to promote mutual understanding among Asian peoples who would be soon in charge of their own destinies.[2] Invitations were sent to political and cultural leaders from 27 countries in North, Southeast, Central, South and West Asia. Australia, the Arab League, Britain, the United Nations and the United States were invited to send observers. The invitations stated that the object of the conference was to promote 'a cultural and political revival, and social progress in Asia, independent of all questions of internal as well as international politics'.[3]

The opening ceremony, on the evening of 23 March 1947, featured a solemn procession of 242 delegates and was attended by some 15,000 people. Standing in front of a huge illuminated map of Asia, Nehru gave the welcoming address, in which he said:

> In this Conference and in this work there are no leaders and no followers. All countries of Asia have to meet together on an equal basis in a common task and equal endeavor. It is fitting that India should play her part in this new phase of Asian development. Apart from the fact that India itself is emerging into freedom and independence, she is the natural centre and focal point of the many forces at work in Asia.[4]

As Nehru warmed to his theme, a frisson of disquiet rippled through the delegates. He began to speak of the broader role of Indian culture in Asia:

streams of culture have flowed from India to distant parts of Asia. If you would know India you would have to go to Afghanistan and Western Asia, to Central Asia, to China and Japan and to the countries of Southeast Asia. There you will find magnificent evidence of the vitality of India's culture which spread out and influenced vast numbers of people.[5]

Nehru's opening speech was not an isolated excursion in Indian cultural chauvinism. When delegates visited the Inter-Asian Art Exhibition held to accompany the conference, they were handed a guide that spoke of an Indian 'cultural empire that once embraced these distant lands for centuries', pointing to Burma, Malaya, Siam, Cambodia, Champa (in modern-day Vietnam) and Indonesia. These unsubtle references called forth a competitive response from the Chinese delegation, represented by members of the beleaguered nationalist Kuomintang government. Soon delegates were being forced to listen to a matching narrative about China's extensive cultural influence across Asia. When, at the end of the conference, the Chinese delegation requested and was awarded the right to host the next Asian Relations Conference, some of the Southeast Asian delegates began to discuss the need for greater subregional solidarity as a way of resisting worrying signs of historical and cultural imperialism on the part of their huge neighbours.[6]

Few remember the Asian Relations Conference, which was completely overshadowed by the Afro-Asian Conference held in Bandung, Indonesia, eight years later – perhaps because so few of those who attended regarded it as a significant event in Asia's postcolonial history. But the further the conference at Purana Qila recedes into the past, the more its cultural tensions and undercurrents seem to have prefigured the contemporary dynamics of confrontation and competition in Asia. For all Asia's diversity, there is a remarkable commonality among its societies, which makes Asia's international relations different from those of any other continent. This is the role of history and culture in Asia's contemporary politics. What the great cultural anthropologist Clifford Geertz wrote of pre-colonial Balinese society can equally be said of most of Asia's contemporary societies: 'the Balinese search the past not so much for the causes of the present as for the standard by which to judge it'.[7] The growing role of civilisational rivalries, and their varied manifestations, is an integral part of interdependence and competition in Asia today. This means that the west's standard ways of thinking about Asia's international relations, which draw exclusively on European history and philosophies, are almost certainly wide of the mark: Asia's future will look nothing like Europe's past. And if we are to understand Asian states and their increasing influence on global affairs, we need to comprehend the roles of hierarchy, history and cultural rivalry that drive and shape the patterns of conflict and competition in Asia.

Hierarchies, Old and New

One thing shared by all societies in Asia is hierarchy. Hierarchy forms the essential structure of Asian societies: it is embedded in relations, in language, in religious cosmology, in moral frameworks, in cultural and social patterns of privilege and deference. Western societies are unequal, but they are founded on norms and expectations of equality; legal systems and democratic politics entrench a presumption of equality of treatment and voice. But however equal or unequal Asian societies are, or at what stage of technological development, or whatever political system they have adopted, hierarchic social structures and mindsets are constantly reproduced. In many cultures there are well-established procedures for working out relative positions in the social hierarchy when strangers first meet; without such a negotiation, appropriate forms of address and communication can't be established. So basic is hierarchy to Asian societies that it dictates how they think about relations within and beyond their own boundaries. Hierarchy forms a moral framework for understanding the world and making it predictable; it is a common logic for ordering and judging relations with compatriots and foreigners alike.

From the earliest recorded history in Asia, hierarchy was the principle used by societies to distinguish themselves from the peoples surrounding them and to tell their own histories. The very concept of 'Chinese-ness' emerged as a sense of cultural superiority to the surrounding 'barbarian' peoples. A sense of cultural uniqueness and superiority is the thread that animates thousands of years of Chinese history; proficiency in Chinese culture was the quality that defined how the Chinese empire classified a people and interacted with it.[8] Hierarchy was established in South and Southeast Asia through the Hindu concept of the mandala – an intricate system of interlocking structures of political and religious authority, all suspended in dynamic relationships of superiority and submission.[9] Thai history, for example, is a chronicle of relations between Thai kings and their neighbours, who are never seen as equals but as either enemies or dependencies.[10] Burma and Vietnam show similar patterns. A strong cosmology underpinned these hierarchical relations: superiority was taken to reflect cultural and moral prestige in a world in which the terrestrial order paralleled the hierarchical divine order. Asia's civilisational hierarchies were exceptionalist and expansionist at the same time: the adoption of religious and political concepts by surrounding societies was taken as evidence of the superiority of one's own culture and religion.

Naturally, a profusion of societies, each believing in its own civilisational superiority, produced dynamism and tension in pre-colonial Asia's international relations. Pragmatism sometimes dictated that a kingdom should defer to a larger neighbour, either in acknowledgement of its greater military power or as a way of legitimising its own claims to authority – or as a way of gaining the right to trade with the larger society. Deference was made easier because its rituals were symbolic, encapsulated in the highly codified practices of paying and acknowledging tribute.[11] Within these rituals, however, was latitude for each side to interpret the relationship in a way that best preserved its own sense of honour and cultural prestige. Larger societies emphasised their civilisational influence on their neighbours, accepting tribute as an acknowledgement of their cultural and moral superiority. Smaller societies often told a very different story, portraying the tributary relationship as one between equals; what appeared to the Chinese emperor as acknowledgement of his superiority was portrayed by the Vietnamese emperor as the mutual acknowledgement of two supreme emperors, each surrounded by a collection of subordinate societies and rulers.[12] Instead of taking cultural borrowings from larger neighbours as evidence of their own inferiority, smaller societies emphasised how these had been adapted and improved in the borrowing. Tension and warfare frequently arose when expectations of deference were not met; failure to properly acknowledge a larger society's superiority was imbued with strong moral judgements, and often followed by wars of punishment designed not to grab territory or gold but to re-establish the appropriate level of deference.

The constant negotiation of international hierarchy and prestige produced much of the dynamism and conflict in pre-colonial Asia. Centuries of contestation produced strong ethnic and cultural stereotypes among neighbouring kingdoms and societies, and out of the struggle for self-respect and prestige within a hierarchical international order emerged strong traditions of national distinctiveness. Vietnam and Korea – despite borrowing heavily from Chinese culture, writing, philosophy and government forms – developed a strong sense of national identity from *not* being Chinese and from their determined resistance to becoming another province of the

Chinese empire.[13] Japan, blessed by its physical separation from the Asian mainland, chose to withdraw itself from the Sinic tributary system, focusing on developing what it saw as its own superior culture and in turn creating its own Japan-centred hierarchical order. Across Southeast Asia and the subcontinent also, a repeated cycle of prestige, resistance, punishment and defiance produced dynamic and ever-changing subsystems of international relations.

When Europeans began to appear from the sea in ever-greater numbers in the sixteenth century, they too were allotted an inferior position in the hierarchies of the societies they encountered. The Europeans appeared uncultured and wanted what Asian societies produced; in return they could offer little that interested the local people other than silver. But two qualities made the Europeans disruptive to Asian hierarchies: their avarice and their military prowess. They were never satisfied with being granted conditional access to Asian economies, and they were brutal and uncompromising in making additional demands. When it was granted, the access was never enough and the coercive diplomacy soon returned. The kingdoms of the subcontinent were the first to make the mistake of thinking that they could harness the savage greed of these interlopers for their own realpolitik purposes; those who started out as allies soon became rapacious and brutal competitors. The kings of the Southeast Asian archipelagos learned the same lesson, but, once again, too late. Over time, the Europeans' coercive avarice became headlong competition to secure exclusive control over and access to the wealth and markets of Asia.

The Europeans who were sent to administer these huge, teeming empires had themselves escaped class-bound hierarchies at home. They, who had suffered the condescension and prejudice of aristocrats, suddenly found themselves all-powerful within Asia's hierarchical societies. The colonialists justified their sudden change in status by developing their own narrative of the cultural and moral superiority of their societies, religion and culture to those of the locals.[14] Overlaying this was a new notion of racial hierarchy, an alchemy of the ancient preoccupation with bloodlines and the newer fascination with biological evolution and the ascent of man. In place of Asia's jostling hierarchies there settled a uniform, suffocating dominance – undeniable in coercive material fact and constantly asserted as the racial, moral and cultural superiority of European over Asian societies. This narrative of racial and cultural superiority, rather than material or coercive preponderance, allowed a handful of Europeans to administer vastly greater numbers of Asians.

To societies that had long considered material and military prowess as evidence of civilisational and moral superiority, the prolonged domination of the Europeans came as a profound psychic shock, one from which Asian societies are yet to recover. Those last to feel the weight of western dominance and condescension – the Japanese, the Koreans and the Chinese – reacted with alarm at the fate of other societies on the continent. Their response to the Europeans' blanket denigration of 'Asians' as an inferior 'race' was to adopt the Europeans' race logic as a way of distinguishing themselves from other subjugated and therefore inferior races.[15] China soon ceased to be the 'significant other' against which Korea and Japan defined their distinctiveness; all three societies became preoccupied with asserting their non-inferiority to the west. But an aspect of pre-colonial Asia's competitive hierarchy remained: in asserting their non-inferiority to the west, many of Asia's subjugated societies continued to distinguish themselves as superior to surrounding societies and cultures.

For those cultures never completely colonised by the west, the newly racialised hierarchy of the colonial system caused a rapid re-evaluation of long-held tributary relationships. What had once been a series of ceremonial and loosely interpreted nominal rankings quickly became relationships of extreme sensitivity to assumptions of superiority and expectations of deference. In 1868, in one of his last decrees, the Thai king Mongkut declared the centuries-old practice of paying tribute to China to be shameful and therefore ordered it abolished.[16] In Japan, a new nativist movement called *kokugaku*, dedicated to denigrating Confucianism and asserting the superiority of Japanese culture and philosophy, gained new momentum in the nineteenth century. Any shoguns of the past, such as Ashikaga Yoshimitsu, who had briefly sent tribute to the Ming emperor's court in return for trading privileges, were denounced.[17] By later in the nineteenth century, Korean reformers denounced as humiliating the practice of *sadae* ('serving the great'), which had long justified Korea's tributary relationship with China. Even today, anti-*sadae*ism provides a highly emotive charge to protests against perceived domination of Korea by the Americans, Chinese or Japanese.

The Europeans and Americans who established dominance over Asia had meanwhile established a system of formal sovereign equality among themselves. But the badge of equality, sovereign statehood, was denied to their colonies. Even those Asian countries that had avoided formal colonisation were denied membership of this club, ostensibly because they failed to meet the required 'standard of civilisation'. It was a standard that rankled with the Japanese, the Thais and the Chinese, all of whom resented being forced to sign treaties imbued with unequal status by various European countries and the United States. The very sovereignty the Europeans and Americans so judiciously accorded each other was cavalierly denied to Asians, whether colonised or not.[18] And in these double standards began to germinate both the intellectual and physical resistance to colonial hierarchy and its justifications – a resistance that made the rule over the many by the few increasingly untenable.

The intellectual and moral justifications of colonialism were shredded by the Nazis' bestial ideology of racial hierarchy and their brutal quest for *lebensraum* in Europe. Condescending racial stereotypes and standards of civilisation became untenable among the coalition of countries resisting Nazism and Japanese militarism. When decolonisation came, it came with a rush, dismantling the colonial order in Asia in just two decades following the end of the Second World War. Complementing the demands of Asians for independence was the intense competition between two anti-colonial superpowers, each vying with the other to present compelling alternative visions of modernity and justice for the postwar world. The ideological competition of the Cold War was total: the United States and the Soviet Union contended for the allegiance of every newly independent or proto-independent state. Every state in Asia – however small, new or impoverished – gained equal sovereign rights, and was treated as such by the competing superpowers and their allies. And so, within decades, Asia's states vaulted from positions of domination and presumed civilisational inadequacy to a situation of radical sovereign equality in which each state, irrespective of size, wealth or internal coherence, became equally important in the ideological rivalry of the superpowers.[19]

Ironically, the new states that had been suddenly pronounced the sovereign equals of their former colonisers were much less certain of their legitimacy within their borders. Most new states simply inherited the boundary demarcations of the colonial era or accepted the hurriedly concocted subdivisions of departing colonial authorities in South Asia, Indochina and West Asia. Many of these new states had not existed as unified political units before the age of colonialism, and within their arbitrary borders were collected random and often antagonistic arrays of ethnicities and religious communities. Sometimes borders divided coherent communities between two or more states. The challenge for Asia's new governments was therefore threefold. They needed to justify their new states as natural expressions of self-determination, rather than the illogical result of some hastily negotiated postcolonial compromise. They had to subsume the great diversities of their populations under an overriding principle of unity, a national essence that drew all communities and confessions together in loyalty to the new state. And they had to conjure a sense of pride and worthiness in their new sovereign status after decades or centuries of material, political and moral subjugation by Europeans.[20]

The response of new state after new state in Asia was to bring the ethnic, religious and linguistic diversity of their population within a broad concept of the civilisational essence that had united the peoples within the state's borders before the Europeans had arrived. India's independence leaders conjured and promoted pride in an Indian civilisation, grounded in Sanskrit cultural traditions and evoked in ancient empires such as that of the Mauryas (322–185 BCE). Indonesia's first president, Sukarno, evoked the great pre-colonial empires of Majapahit (1293–1500 CE) and Srivijaya (seventh–eleventh century CE) to justify the unity of a vast archipelago stretching from Aceh to Papua.[21] The new Cambodian state chose to put on its flag a picture of the huge temple complex of Angkor Wat, a monument to the glory of the Khmer empire during the twelfth century. In China, the unity of the state was never in doubt, but the urge to assert civilisational greatness and privileges beyond its borders proved strong. After the overthrow of the Qing Dynasty, China's nationalists reacted to China's humiliation at the hands of imperialist powers by referring to former tributary relationships with Laos, Vietnam, Burma and Korea as 'lost colonies'.[22] But these societies conjuring pre-colonial civilisational greatness held on with equal passion to a conviction that was very much a product of the colonial age: that deference and subjugation are shameful.

The result has been a gradual re-emergence into Asia's postcolonial international relations of many of the hierarchical pretensions and resistances of Asia's pre-colonial times. Across Asia resonate concentric and overlapping expectations of deference and sensitivities to hierarchy, forming a constant undercurrent of regional relations all the more profound for regional leaders' attempts to conceal them behind displays of bonhomie. Over decades, prejudices and antagonisms have only been heightened by the bursts of economic development that temporarily distinguish countries from their neighbours, and by the political capital that becomes invested in these differential growth rates. The length of tenure of many of the region's leaders, and the deep investment of elites in the state's economic fortunes, tends only to further personalise judgements of success and superiority.

A complex set of jealousies underlies relations between Singapore and its neighbours. As a small Chinese-majority state that enjoyed spectacular economic success before any of its larger Malay-majority neighbours, Singapore is the constant focus of suspicion. Malaysia, the country that expelled Singapore from its body politic in 1965, is particularly thin-skinned when it comes to any sense of superiority or condescension. Singapore reciprocates with its own great sensitivity to any sign of being treated by Malaysia on *adang-aduk* (big brother–little brother) lines.[23] Some of these jealousies began to subside in the mid-1980s as the Malaysian economy began to develop rapidly. But they returned abruptly as the Asian financial crisis ripped great holes in the Malaysian economy. Prime Minister Mahathir accused Singapore of manipulating the value of the Malaysian ringgit and disrupting the stock exchange with the intent of keeping Malaysia poor and subservient.

Kuala Lumpur, meanwhile, fears being forced to play the *aduk* to a neighbouring *adang* – Indonesia. Despite regular protestations of Malay fraternity, relations between Indonesia and Malaysia are pervaded with mutual negative stereotypes. Suffusing Indonesia's sense of self is an awareness of size and historical greatness, of being the greatest representative of the Malay peoples, and pride in its violent struggle for independence. To Malaysians these self-perceptions are presumptuous and condescending, particularly given that their country, while it never struggled for independence, has preserved its Malay royalty and nobility in continuity with pre-colonial Malay society. Indonesians living in Malaysia confront everyday prejudices that cast them as the source of crime and disease. Relations between Jakarta and Kuala Lumpur become particularly strained at times when Malaysia becomes assertive regionally and internationally. Indonesia reacted angrily when Dr Mahathir proposed a new regional grouping, the East Asian Economic Group (EAEG), in 1990. Indonesia's elites interpreted the scheme as a usurpation of Indonesia's regional leadership role and muttered that Mahathir's combative style was simply not the way things were done in Southeast Asia. The Malaysian media, in response, interpreted Indonesia's opposition to the EAEG as the manifestation of a deeper drive to dominate Malaysia and all of Southeast Asia.[24]

Indonesia, a country that assumes a natural leadership in Southeast Asia and reacts defensively to any perceived challenge, is itself highly sensitive to any presumption of superiority by larger Asian states. Foreign Minister Ali Alatas was at great pains to assert the equality of Indonesia and China at the time of the normalisation of their relations in 1990:

> China, no matter what, is a big country. It is big in terms of its population; it plays a big role as a developing country. So is Indonesia. We live in the same region. And, this region is experiencing turbulence, in the process of rapid change. Indonesia and China are two most active and important actors.[25]

China's rapid rise, from a marginalised small economy to the largest and most central economy in the region, has led to heightened attentiveness among a range of countries to any assertions of superiority from Beijing. When Chinese Foreign Minister Yang Jiechi exploded in frustration at ASEAN states' criticism of Beijing's actions in the South China Sea, telling Singaporean Foreign Minister George Yeo, 'China is a big country and other countries are small countries, and that's just a fact',[26] the remark echoed around the region. Concerns voiced in Vietnam, Korea, the Philippines and Malaysia sound remarkably similar: the rise of 'great Han nationalism' in China aims to use wealth and power to place other countries in a deferential relationship.[27]

The highly politicised and sensitive place of culture and history in Asia means that 'soft power', the use of moral and cultural attraction to advance foreign policy outcomes, is stillborn among Asian states. Societies fear that cultural admiration will be taken as an acknowledgement of cultural inferiority. For many years, Seoul blocked the broadcasting of Japanese pop culture in South Korea out of fear that it would undermine Korean cultural traditions and subordinate the country to Japan. A growing number of Vietnamese worry about China's expanding economic, political and cultural influence over their country. The media and popular culture are increasingly playing roles in the assertion of their societies' intrinsic value and authenticity, and in their defence against other societies' pretensions of superiority.

History's Futures

In the steamy July of 2004, South Korea's bustling capital, Seoul, ignited in a burst of collective anger. Bemused visitors watched television news channels covering widespread protests: young South Koreans dressed in historical costumes chanting slogans at the Chinese embassy; internet activists calling themselves *euibyong*, after ancient Korean guerrillas who fought Chinese and Japanese invaders, demanding boycotts of Chinese goods and tourism; a young demonstrator tearing up a Chinese flag with his teeth and spitting it on the ground. A poll published by the *Korea Herald* the following month showed that the proportion of South Korean National Assembly members who believed China to be South Korea's most important diplomatic partner in Asia had fallen to 6 per cent from 63 per cent four months previously.[28]

To most observers, South Korea's plummeting regard for China came as an abrupt reversal. In the decade after the normalisation of Sino-South Korean relations, bilateral trade had expanded tenfold and China had become South Korea's largest trading partner. Some of South Korea's industrial *chaebols* were well on their way to becoming the largest single investors in the Chinese economy. Chinese people had become eager consumers of the 'Korean wave' of popular culture, while young South Koreans studying in China had topped 30,000 and were rising. Some in Washington had begun to ask whether South Korea was slowly abandoning its commitment to its American alliance and drifting gradually into China's orbit.

The cause of South Korean anger was a story in China's *People's Daily* reporting UNESCO's listing of Koguryo (37 BCE – 688 CE) as a World Heritage site in which it was referred to the 'ancient Koguryo kingdom of China'. To South Koreans, such a claim struck at the core of their national identity: their national and ethnic name was derived from Koguryo and all South Koreans had been raised on stories of bold Koguryo warriors fighting off Chinese invaders. Now, a new 'Northeast History Project' launched by the Chinese Academy of Social Sciences claimed Koguryo as a regional province of the Chinese empire.[29] Among its historians were those promoting a legend that Korea was founded by a Chinese prince called Jizi and that most of the Koguryo kingdom, including its capital for 460 of its 725 years, lay in modern-day China. Even more galling for South Koreans, the Chinese Foreign Ministry had removed all mention of Koguryo from the summary of Korean history on the Republic of Korea page of its website.

Despite the visit of Chinese Vice Minister of Foreign Affairs Wu Dawei to Seoul in August 2004 to calm the dispute, it was clear that China was not resiling from its claim. In December, it issued postage stamps commemorating the UNESCO World Heritage listing of Koguryo sites. The excision of Koguryo from the Foreign Ministry website wasn't reversed – instead *all* references to Korean history were removed. Anger and suspicion among South Koreans continued. Historical dramas set in a clearly Korean Koguryo began to dominate South Korean television. The government in Seoul launched its own Koguryo Research Foundation, to be renamed the Northeast Asian History Foundation in 2006. In 2005, North and South Korean archaeologists launched a joint project to study Koguryo-era burial mounds near Pyongyang – the first-ever joint research project between two countries still formally at war.

The South Korean newspapers competed to editorialise about Beijing's motives for stealing their history. For some, it was a strategy to perpetuate Korea's division into north and south. By appropriating Koguryo, the Chinese were denying the essential historical unity of the Korean Peninsula, conceding that only kingdoms that occupied the peninsula's south were authentically Korean. Others discerned an even more imperialist intent. South Koreans of all walks of life bristled at the underlying implication that their country's long and proud history was derivative of China's. Some editorials warned of a campaign by Beijing to subject Korea to a new subordinate relationship in which an increasingly tributary economic relationship would shade into an assumption that the Korean Peninsula was simply one of China's provinces. Some commentators pointed out that China's claim to Koguryo history might have been a defensive reaction to Beijing's fears that its heavily ethnic-Korean-populated northeastern provinces could begin agitating for separation from the People's Republic.[30] But this interpretation did little to assuage the resentment and suspicion of most South Koreans.

To westerners, the Koguryo controversy is hard to understand. The equivalent dispute in the west would be tension between Italy and Greece over whether the early Byzantine empire was Latin or Greek. That this is unimaginable shows that, for westerners, history is an ever-receding sequence of events of contemporary interest that give the lineage of current affairs or provide a source of compelling narratives or moral lessons. Rarely is such ancient history the cause of public passions or national antagonisms, or interpreted as central to contemporary international relations.

Such disputes over history, ancient and modern, are strewn across Asia. Koreans and Japanese argue passionately over whether the martial art kendo and the traditional tea ceremony originated in Korea or Japan.[31] Indonesians and Malaysians disagree over where batik and wayang puppetry originated. Chinese anger at Japanese textbook interpretations of history goes back to 1910 – and continues to colour bilateral relations over a century later.[32] For almost as long, Koreans have taken exception to the claims in the same textbooks that Japan has exercised influence over Korea since ancient times.

Across Asia, national histories are never allowed to recede. They are regularly invoked as talismans of national pride and authenticity. Asian histories glower over the present, imposing lenses for interpreting current affairs, holding aloft ideals of political power and cultural glory towards which peoples aspire, constantly throwing up causes to be defended against the claims of others. This is not new. Before the colonial era, the writing of history was central to the practice of foreign policy; Thai kings and Vietnamese emperors alike were as attentive to the interpretation of events in their official histories as they were to the actual conduct of affairs with foreign kingdoms.[33] Today, the standards of history are no less demanding.

What one scholar observes of China could equally be said of other elites in Asia:

> Chinese governments have, for at least 2000 years, taken history much too seriously to allow the future to make its own unguided judgements about them ... The religion of the Chinese ruling classes is the Chinese state, and it is through history that the object of devotion is to be understood.[34]

Asian states' historical consciousness provides complex sets of stereotypes and narrative structures for interpreting the present. The court histories of past Thai kings inform contemporary Thai stereotypes about neighbouring societies and form a moral framework for Bangkok's contemporary regional relations. Despite the recent warming of bilateral relations, the Thai stereotype of Myanmar is that of a wicked and implacable enemy; its colonisation by Britain is interpreted as punishment for its wickedness, while Thailand's freedom from colonisation is taken to attest to its virtue and wisdom. Laos and Cambodia were seen by Thailand as inferior, untrustworthy and ungrateful for Thailand's benevolence; Phnom Penh's claiming of Angkor Wat as a totem of a great Cambodian past is a source of irritation to Thais. The Malay states to the south were seen as sources of tribute, to be watched closely and treated harshly if they misbehaved. Vietnam is to be watched as a potential threat, forgetful of Thailand's support in its struggle against China and covetous of Thailand's natural sphere of influence over Laos and Cambodia.[35]

Historical scripts heavily influence how contemporary events are interpreted. China's launching of punitive attacks on India in 1962 and Vietnam in 1979 were widely seen in the region as a return to old patterns of behaviour, when the Chinese empire would launch wars of punishment against kingdoms believed to be insufficiently deferential. After invading Cambodia in late 1978, Vietnam reverted to pre-colonial patterns of administering conquered neighbours, instituting a suzerain relationship rather than directly annexing Cambodian territory. Indonesia and Thailand interpreted the developing Sino-Vietnamese confrontation in mainland Southeast Asia according to their own histories of resisting China's domination; Jakarta was to remain sympathetic to Hanoi's position, which it saw as an entirely understandable assertion of independence from China's influence.[36] Thailand saw the same events very differently – its historical scripts conjured memories of an ungrateful and covetous Vietnam ever willing to encroach on Thailand's natural sphere of influence.[37] Bangkok became the most vigorous opponent of Vietnam's suzerainty over Cambodia.

Dangerous Mosaics

In today's world, multicultural societies are the norm. It is quicker to list ethnically or religiously homogeneous societies than heterogeneous societies, and even these lists have to be qualified. In Asia, Korea, Mongolia and Japan stand out as ethnically homogeneous, even though contemporary South Korea and Japan host growing minorities from elsewhere in Asia. The other states of Asia are shot through with ethnic and religious diversity. While many modern states view their diversity as source of strength and enrichment, ethnic and religious diversity in Asia is more often than not a cause of antagonism and anxiety. In most Asian states, heterogeneity is seen as a potential source of fragility, and, for many, fears about internal minorities run parallel with and play into fears about external aggression and domination.

Asia's complex ethnic and religious mosaics are the result of centuries of social sedimentation left behind by the tides of conflict, commerce and colonialism. The political map of pre-colonial

Asia was shaped and reshaped by the sequential rise and fall of kingdoms and empires. Unlike in Europe, these had no defined and mutually exclusive boundaries – Asia's kingdoms were more like circular force fields in which power, authority and submission radiated outwards from the court, becoming gradually weaker the further one travelled from the capital. When one kingdom invaded another in mainland Southeast Asia, it tended to seize people rather than territory, marching thousands of captured slaves back to its own territories. Rarely did a political order last long; surrounding tribes were, in Clifford Geertz's words, 'only reluctantly subservient ... loyal when necessary, rebellious when possible'.[38] As a result, outside the more permanent empires lay large tracts of political marchlands, inhabited by peoples rarely subject to political authority, occasionally acknowledging a distant court but largely left alone to nurture local traditions, bloodlines, languages and beliefs.

The exceptions, of course, were the great empires of China and the Mughals. The boundaries of the Chinese empire pressed outwards over thousands of years from its beginnings in the Yellow River valley, in the process subjecting a large array of ethnic groups and religions to imperial rule. But imperial China was never able to impose ethnic or linguistic unity on its new subjects. Despite their acculturation to the Chinese writing system, Confucian moral concepts and Chinese literary traditions, populations outside the heartland maintained mutually incomprehensible languages and held firm to distinctive ethnic identities and cultural traditions.[39] Some – such as the Vietnamese, Koreans and Burmese – defined their identity against an ethnic and cultural Chinese-ness and fought for their independence despite repeated invasions and incursions. The great conquests of the Qing Dynasty in the eighteenth century, which nearly doubled the size of the Chinese empire, absorbed peoples with fierce pride in their ethnic history, strong memories of their own empire-building and deep commitment to strong transnational religions.

In the subcontinent, the Mughal Empire presided over an even more complex patchwork of ethnic groups, languages and religions. Despite being the South Asian front of Islam's conquests across the known world, the early Mughal conquerors were remarkably tolerant of the religious diversity they found south of the Himalayas. Emperor Akbar took a deep interest in the religions of the subcontinent and promulgated a synthesis between Islam and Hindu theologies and traditions.[40] His much more doctrinaire great-grandson Aurangzeb took the Mughal Empire's borders to their greatest limits, subjecting all of modern India save its southern tip to Mughal rule, but his more uncompromising approach of imposing Muslim orthodoxy on his subjects was no more successful than Akbar's approach in bringing homogeneity to India.

Adding to all these social complexities were the powerful veins of commerce that connected and coursed through pre-colonial Asian societies. As historian Anthony Reid has shown, maritime Asia was a commercial domain every bit as vigorous as the Mediterranean before the Europeans arrived.[41] The result was the establishment over centuries of trading communities drawn from across Asia in the major entrepot ports: Indians and Arabs on the China coast; Indians, Chinese and Arabs through the Indonesian archipelago; Chinese and Arabs around the coasts of the subcontinent. Some societies absorbed these minorities over time through intermarriage and acculturation; in others, no amount of intermarriage and acculturation would convince the locals to assimilate these trading communities.

On the winds of trade came the seeds of new religions: Buddhism, Islam and eventually Christianity. Some grew strongly in the local soil, gaining followers rapidly, especially if the king converted, and often being modified to accommodate local religious traditions. In other places the religions stuck in some communities but not others, occasionally even provoking the resurgence of local beliefs. Sometimes, confessional roots grew deeply where they spoke to a spiritual, social or political need; elsewhere, the roots were shallow, going no further than prescribing rituals and proprieties necessary to gain certain commercial privileges.

It was onto these complex mandalas that the European colonialists imposed the mutually exclusive territorial boundaries they had pioneered in Europe. Suddenly, Asia's extensive marchland communities were subject to constant and enduring rule, often dragooned into alien extraction and production systems, and harangued by judgemental and uncompromising missionaries. Boundaries between colonies reflected not any natural discontinuities among societies, religions and ethnicities, but the place where one avaricious power urge fought or negotiated another to a standstill.

Onto this arbitrary division and conglomeration of languages, beliefs and peoples, the colonial age gave rise to new flows of people between societies in Asia. The wobbling Qing empire bled thousands of impoverished people from southern China into Southeast Asia, while the increasingly assertive British Empire emboldened thousands of South Asians to fan out across the Bay of Bengal.[42] The beliefs and demands of imperialism led to further migrations. The ideology of race hierarchy convinced colonial administrators not only of their own superiority to all Asians, but also of a rough hierarchy among Asians as well. While some ethnic groups were stereotyped as enterprising and efficient, others were seen as indolent and untrustworthy. Plantations and mines needed hardworking coolies; commercial hubs needed entrepreneurial merchants; colonial administration needed conscientious mandarins.[43] New migrations of 'favoured' groups – Vietnamese into Cambodia and Laos, Chinese into the Dutch East Indies, Chinese and Indians into British Malaya and Burma – were sponsored by the colonial authorities, their implicit critique of the locals and favoured treatment by the Europeans planting the seeds of long-term resentments.

The waning of the colonial empires in Asia left this social complexity in its backwash.[44] Imperialism's racial categories had given inter-ethnic relations a judgemental edge that they have never lost, and the ideal of the nation-state they inherited made postcolonial governments deeply anxious about the heterogeneous societies they had to forge into coherent states. The response of many was to try to impose a uniformity around a core ethnic identity: Khin in Vietnam, Malay in Malaysia, Burman in Myanmar, Thai, Cambodian and Lao. Their answer was to tie the identity of the state firmly to the language and religion of the core ethnicity, either imposing these on minority communities or excluding them from economic and political power – ultimately only deepening intercommunal resentments.[45] Some, such as Indonesia and India, opted for an ideology of diversity, but soon found themselves under trenchant critique from dominant religious communities, who often vented their frustrations on minorities.

Within a generation, most of Asia's states had succumbed to serious communal violence. The embers of the holocaust of Hindu-Muslim bloodletting that accompanied partition in India in 1947 continued to burst aflame, horrifying the world with the shocking cruelty of the Gujarat riots of 2002. Chinese communities fled Hanoi's conquest of all of Vietnam, and Vietnamese minorities fled the murderous Khmer Rouge in Cambodia. A military coup targeting the Indonesian Communist Party unleashed a pogrom against the Chinese minority that claimed hundreds of thousands of lives. Increasingly ethnically polarised voting in Malaysia exploded into deadly communal riots.[46] Sri Lanka plunged into a brutal civil war that devoured thousands of lives over decades, only to be ended by even greater heights of brutality. Tibet and Xinjiang were regularly convulsed with violent protests over Beijing's rule and the growing influx of Han Chinese migrants.

The legacy of this suspicion and unrest has been an enduring anxiety about internal fragility among most states in Asia. In the aftermath of its coup, Indonesia banned the use of Chinese language or writing and suppressed all Chinese festivals. Thailand forced its Chinese and Muslim minorities to adopt Thai names and learn the Thai language. Post-riot Malaysia installed a new political compact designed to deflate all hope of political power for its Chinese and Indian minorities, while providing a generous system of affirmative action for ethnic Malays.[47] Singapore developed immigration policies designed to maintain the Chinese community as the overwhelming majority. Both Malaysia and Singapore enacted draconian internal security laws to guard against dissent. For much of their first half century, Asia's new militaries – and paramilitaries – trained their guns inwards, ready to quash any new round of ethnic unrest. Indonesia's army codified its role as *dwifungsi* – dual-functioned – explicitly linking the tasks of national defence and internal stabilisation.[48] The Thai and Philippine militaries periodically carried out brutal operations against their southern Muslim minorities. Myanmar has fought almost non-stop against its internal ethnic minorities.

But while the guns may have been trained inwards, ethnic suspicion linked internal mistrust with external anxieties. Although Asia's diasporas had travelled and settled in different countries, they maintained strong emotional attachments to their homelands. Foremost were ethnic Chinese communities in Southeast Asia. China's 1895 defeat by Japan galvanised the communities into agitating for the overthrow of the Qing Dynasty in China as the best way of meeting the challenge of Meiji Japan.[49] Familial and business networks turned easily into political secret societies, and Sun Yat-sen and other republican reformers were funded, nurtured and protected by the Chinese diaspora. This new activism, combined with the often close working relationships between Chinese minorities and colonial administrations, led to deep suspicions of minorities among local populations. It meant that when the Japanese army swept through Southeast Asia in 1942, local populations were both eager and passive supporters of the occupying army's mistreatment of ethnic Chinese communities.

With the defeat of Japan in 1945, Chinese minorities in Asia continued to be politically active. The beleaguered Kuomintang government of Chiang Kai-shek reactivated its links with Southeast Asian Chinese communities, many of whom contributed financially to Chiang's struggle against the communists. With Mao's victory in China in 1949, the new People's Republic bent its energies towards reorienting Chinese diasporas away from Chiang's nationalists and towards support for the new government of China. Beijing chose for its ambassador to Jakarta the Indonesian Chinese Wang Ren-shu, who energetically engaged with Chinese communities across Indonesia.[50] In Malaya in the 1950s, many in the Chinese community were grateful for Beijing's support in the increasingly bitter tussle with the Malay community over the shape of an independent Malaya. Consequently, many of the Communist guerillas fighting the Malayan insurgency were ethnically Chinese. In the febrile atmosphere of the early–Cold War and postcolonial state-building, pointed questions began to be asked about whether ethnic minorities were loyal to the new state or to some external power with nefarious designs on the fledgling state.

External anxieties and domestic antagonisms fed into each other. In Indonesia, President Sukarno's growing closeness to Beijing in the early 1960s made his opponents in the military increasingly paranoid about the Indonesian Communist Party and its predominantly Chinese membership. Indonesia and Malaysia, both deeply anxious about the Chinese within, often focused their animosity on the Chinese outside: Singapore in their own region and China further afield.[51] Singapore mirrored their fears, its unease about its two larger Malay neighbours often translating into a distrust of its Malay minority internally. Singapore continues to tread carefully in formulating its policy towards Beijing for fear of stirring up the paranoia of Indonesia and Malaysia. Further north, as recent anxiety grows in Vietnam about China's assertiveness and growing regional influence, a new round of 'othering' and persecution has begun against Vietnam's remaining ethnic Chinese minority.[52]

Internal–external ethnic anxieties are not only concentrated on the Chinese. Often Jakarta's worries about the cohesion of the Indonesian state feed into suspicions of both Singapore and Malaysia. Singapore's entrepot economy, which for centuries has animated trading networks into Sumatra, is seen by many in Jakarta as a parasitic, centrifugal influence on the cohesion of the Indonesian economy.[53] For decades, Indonesia has watered down or opposed ASEAN plans for greater regional integration because of its deep anxieties about its own cohesion and coherence in the face of transnational economic forces. Sumatra also lies at the heart of Indonesia's suspicions of Malaysia. The separation of Sumatra from peninsular Malaysia by an 1824 colonial subdivision and then a sovereign border has not diluted the close cultural and ethnic ties between Malay communities on both sides of the Strait of Malacca. Many in Jakarta worry that Kuala Lumpur manipulates these links and fans resentment against Javanese domination as a way of weakening Indonesia and drawing Sumatra towards Malaysia. Indonesians with long memories recall Malaysia's sympathy for internal rebellions in Indonesia in the late 1950s and its ambivalence over Indonesia's claims to West Irian.[54]

Such patterns of internal–external anxieties lead to different levels of paranoia about encirclement by hostile forces in many Asian countries. Indonesia's President Sukarno reacted with alarm to the establishment of a unified Malaya when the British withdrew in 1957. In launching military action against the new state, Sukarno believed Indonesia needed to prevent the consolidation of a surrounding, smothering, western-leaning entity hostile to Indonesia.[55] His successor, Suharto, became nervous when Malaysia and Singapore signed the Five Power Defence Arrangements with Britain,

Australia and New Zealand: once again Indonesia was being surrounded by a potentially hostile coalition. In its recent disputes with
China over the South China Sea, Vietnam fears it is being enveloped
and isolated by its northern neighbour. Not only do Chinese claims
threaten Vietnam's access to the sea, but China's growing sway over
Hanoi's landward neighbours Cambodia and Laos also appears to
many Vietnamese to portend a threatening encirclement.[56] While
Indonesia and Malaysia often draw close together at times of heightened fear of China, Singapore looks to external partners – such as
Taiwan and Australia – as a source of 'strategic depth' against a possible encircling coalition of its two neighbours.

For its part, China worries constantly about 'containment' by
hostile neighbours backed by the United States, eyeing increasingly
cordial relations among Japan, India, Vietnam and Australia with
concern. India has its own encirclement fears. Long paranoid about
the Sino-Pakistani alignment, it watches closely how its neighbours
to the north and east – Myanmar, Bangladesh, Nepal and Bhu-
tan – manage their relations with Beijing.[57] Meanwhile, the belief
that China is constructing a maritime 'string of pearls' consisting
of naval bases across the Indian Ocean has great currency in New
Dehli. Japan and South Korea also have their own isolation anxieties: Tokyo worries about being left alone to face an ascendant
China; Seoul about its own friendless neighbourhood.

History, hierarchy and culture, mixed with rapid economic
development, combine to make Asia's states restless souls. The
never-healing wounds of western subjugation, plus the need to
build cohesion among and attachment of diverse societies to their
new states, drive them to be culturally and politically assertive and
often prickly about what they perceive to be others' presumptions.
But this plays badly with their neighbours, prompting an assertive
and prickly response in turn. It means that the sedimentation of distrust and rivalry continues to build within and between Asia's states.

It means that no amount of regionalism will wipe away long-held stereotypes, and that even minor issues – a World Heritage listing here, a cultural festival there – can excite animosities and suspicions remarkably quickly.

5

FATEFUL TERRAINS

Local legend has it that a Hindu prince named Parameswara, escaping an attack on the island kingdom of Singapura by the Javanese Majapahit Empire, collapsed with exhaustion under a wild gooseberry tree on the banks of a wide bay. As he gathered his breath, he noticed his hunting dogs had cornered a small mouse-deer. In an act of desperation, the mouse-deer charged the dogs, so startling them that they fell into the bay, allowing the deer to escape. Parameswara took this as an omen that the weak may defeat the strong, and decided to found a great city on that spot. He named the city after the tree he'd sheltered under: Melaka.

By fate or wisdom, Parameswara had chosen an auspicious spot. The bay was an all-weather harbour, located at the narrowest point of the straits separating the island of Sumatra from the Malay Peninsula. Parameswara and his successors offered dependable port facilities and reliable warehousing to the sailors who plied the straits, and soon Melaka became a thriving, cosmopolitan hub on a vigorous maritime trading highway that stretched from the Japanese islands to the Persian Gulf and beyond to Europe. Melaka was an ideal location for the Indian and Burmese traders who rode the Bay of Bengal monsoon rhythms to tranship goods to the Malay and Chinese ships that were more familiar with the South China Sea's moods. In playing this role, Melaka joined a string of transshipment ports, such as Cochin in India and Muscat in the Gulf, along that great commercial thoroughfare. Always with an eye to commercial advantage, Parameswara's descendants converted to Islam in the fourteenth century to attract more Arab, Gujarati and Bengali traders, and Sultan Mansur Shah is even said to have married a Ming Dynasty princess in the mid-fifteenth century to shore up commercial relations with the Celestial Empire.[1]

Neither commercial shrewdness nor the omen of the plucky mouse-deer were much help when a flotilla of Portuguese men-of-war under the command of buccaneer admiral Afonso de Albuquerque sailed down the straits in August 1511. Albuquerque had already conquered Muscat and Goa; to his mind there was much to be gained for his king from establishing Portuguese control over all of the hubs of the lucrative maritime trading highway. Melaka resisted Albuquerque's first onslaught but succumbed to his second. The Portuguese spared all Hindu, Chinese and Burmese traders in the city but killed or sold into servitude all Muslims.[2] Many of these slaves helped to build a red stone fort on a small hill overlooking the harbour and stud its ramparts with cannons.

Just over a century later, Melaka surrendered after a brutal six-month siege to the Dutch and their ally the sultan of Johor. The capture of Melaka heralded an era of Dutch primacy in the Indian and Pacific oceans – and the end of the Portuguese. The Dutch held the port for a century and a half before it was seized by the British, taking advantage of Napoleon's invasion of the Netherlands in 1795. The British retained Melaka under the terms of the 1824 Anglo-Dutch Treaty, in exchange for the Sumatran city of Bencoolen.[3] Melaka's role as a trade hub slowly declined as Singapore's grew; today it is a vibrant cosmopolitan tourist hub, gazing serenely out on the straits that borrowed its name.

Melaka's turbulent career shows how central geography is to history. History swarmed around this port, as it has around other points of the earth's surface – the Levant, the Bosporus, the Hindu Kush, the Low Countries – with much greater intensity than over other parts. Certain formations of land and water seem to channel human traffic and engage human avarice through the centuries, and over these terrains are steadily etched corridors of blood and treasure.

Geography is to states what DNA is to humans: an inescapable legacy that enables, shapes and limits their potential and pathologies. For humans – the most intensely territorial and competitive of animals – power, wealth, safety, order and creativity are all played out across the medium of geography. Humans have organised into exclusive communities each with its own territory, which provides each society a unique fingerprint of landforms and water domains: coasts, ranges, plains, islands, deserts, volcanos, deltas, forests and valleys. Onto the earth's surface, the human mind has painted panoramas of fear, greed and pride. Each society's territory carries with it a quantum of opportunity and vulnerability, as assessed by the fervid imaginations of its inhabitants and competitors.[4] It is the lucrative or dangerous potential of some landforms to the human mind that draws history so intensely to some parts of the earth's surface while leaving others touched only by the elements.

Over millennia, human territoriality and strategic imagination have become bound in a tightening spiral, each intensifying the other. Five hundred years ago, in the verdant valleys between the Pacific and Indian oceans, kings fought for people, not land. In the periodic wars between Siamese and Burmese, victors marched away with thousands of slaves, leaving the land they invaded devastated but not occupied. An empire's power was measured by the loyalties it commanded, not the land it controlled.[5] Asia's empires were like solar systems whose power gradually waned the further one travelled from the rules, wealth and learning of the imperial capital.

On the other side of the earth, in Europe, a more intense alchemy between terrain and imagination was emerging. For a thousand years after the collapse of Rome, Europeans claimed and defended territory from empires down to clans and families in an elaborate tapestry of ascending and overlapping claims of loyalty and authority. But under the combined assault of military technology and religious schism, the tapestry was to be rewoven into much starker simple patterns.[6] Europe's political map was redrawn into exclusive territorial holdings, each imbued with a growing national consciousness, at the same moment that Europe's restless energy burst forth from that continent.

Europeans carried the spirit of their territorial competitiveness to their colonisation of the Americas, Asia and Africa. Holdings that began as trading concessions metastasised into exclusive territorial possessions in the heat of rivalries with other European empires. Sometimes the boundaries drawn between empires followed the principles of demarcation in Europe: in modern geographers' jargon, either physiographic (using natural dividers such as ranges or rivers) or anthropomorphic (following ethnic, religious or linguistic cleavages).[7] But more often they were geometric – arbitrary lines drawn on a map – dividing communities and uniting 'unalikes' out of a mixture of imperial lassitude, ignorance and rivalry.

So a regime of absolute exclusive boundaries supplanted Asia's system of ambiguous, shifting and sometimes overlapping frontiers. Asian aspirations for independence and redemption took on the exclusive territorial grammar of colonial subjugation. The states that emerged from the collapse of empires inherited and squabbled over the boundaries the Europeans had drawn. In Asia, as in the other continents, the imperatives of exclusive territoriality concentrated states' most sensitive nerve endings along their borders. To societies that had experienced domination by the progressive loss of territory to creeping empires, the ability to hold, defend and reclaim territory – however rebellious, remote or barren – became a talisman of effectiveness and respect. Borders became the front lines in the campaigns for authority of Asia's new states. It was over borders that territorial disputes raged and festered, across which insurgencies oozed and armies burst, and within which governments tried to build national communities and integrate national economies.

As Asia's borders hardened, so a closed system of exclusive territoriality emerged across the earth's inhabited surface. It was a system in which, the great geographer Sir Halford Mackinder pointed out, there was no longer any ambiguous space to absorb tensions and shocks – which could quickly reverberate well beyond their original location.[8] The regime of sovereign states had two components: a general set of ordering principles governing the terms of division of territory, and the actual distribution of ownership and use of territory among states. In Asia, both elements have always been subject to dispute. The actual distribution of land and water is subject to multiple disagreements, while in the heat of the prosecution of claims, the principles of distribution are often in dispute.[9]

This discussion of humans' territorial competitiveness may seem out of place in this age of global corporations, planetary warming and cheap, near-seamless international travel and communications. But pronouncements of the death of geography are considerably premature. They overlook the countless lives lost, atrocities committed and communities uprooted in the name of defining, disputing or defending territory. Or how vigorously any state will defend its borders when they are challenged. Contrary to our deepest hopes for human advancement, the rules, demarcations and understandings that define our world sit on the foundations of a structure of latent violence. In the words of Nobel laureate Thomas Schelling, 'like the threat of a strike in industrial relations, the threat of divorce in a family dispute, or the threat of bolting the party at a political convention, the threat of violence continuously circumscribes international politics.'[10]

The great Prussian strategist Carl von Clausewitz famously argued that war is a continuation of policy by other means[11] – but the opposite claim is equally true. All policy – what governments are able to do within but particularly beyond their borders – is enabled or prevented by an underlying distribution or structure of latent force. International relations is ultimately a shared web of explicit and implicit understandings about what is and is not permissible, as defined by a substructure of understandings about what can and will be enforced or defended and what can be credibly challenged without risking self-defeating damage.

This underlying structure of violence is now mostly kept sublimated – unlike in most human history, when the cycle of wars among states was a regular heartbeat in the passing of time. Two twentieth-century developments have forced violence into latency: economic interdependence and nuclear weapons. Violence is no longer the regrettable cost of high statecraft. The violence that even moderately sized countries can now inflict can cause catastrophic damage to the economic viability of purveyors, opponents and bystanders alike. The escalation of conflict to the level of a nuclear exchange could eliminate all life on the planet. In our world of diversity and rivalry, one interest all societies share is to avoid catastrophic, self-defeating, all-in war.[12]

But as even casual observers of international affairs will point out, this has not banished from our world either the use or threat of violence or the laying in of its means. Within the shared framework of common interests in avoiding catastrophic war lies ample room to threaten or deploy coercive power. In this age of constrained conflict, the tools of statecraft have become highly creative in developing forms of subtly implied violence and non-forceful coercion that still draw on common understandings of the distribution of force. The acme of statecraft lies in judging how much coercion can be deployed or implied, and in what form, to secure the state's goals without triggering a broader, catastrophic conflict. In a world of diverse interests and endlessly evolving power relativities, states dissatisfied with the current rules and institutions must carefully judge how forceful their challenge can be; just as those determined to maintain the status quo must judge how vigorous they can be in resisting such challenges. Deprived of the option of a culminating contest of arms over rules and distributions of territories, twenty-first century states occupy a fog-bound world of careful probing, sequential accretions and implicit bargaining over rights and interests.

The sheer scale and scope of economic growth in Asia means that across the world's largest continent the most intense contests over rules, principles and territorial possessions are occurring. Paradoxically, when they were at their weakest, Asian states articulated their ambitions in global terms: from global revolution to non-alignment. Now, as they rise, their security ambitions and fears have begun to regionalise closer to home. A combination of anxieties is at work: awareness of their neighbours' growing military capabilities; a sense of vulnerability due to their expanding dependence on outside markets, resources and energy; and the need to demonstrate that with power and wealth comes respect. A distinctly Asian version of what security scholar John Herz dubbed the 'security dilemma'[13] has developed: countries worried about encirclement or containment by their rivals seek alignments and build infrastructure to forestall such strategies, but in the process they aggravate others' fears of encirclement or containment. What appears defensive in one capital looks menacing in another. Asia's landforms and waterscapes offer multiple and overlapping combinations of threats and promise, driving the strategic imaginations and military acquisitions of its countries, large and small.

Asia's Strategic Geographies

Seen from a satellite, the continent of Asia forms an untidy, slightly elongated square, stretching approximately 8700 kilometres from the Mediterranean Sea to the Pacific, and about 9700 kilometres from the Arctic to the Indian Ocean. Within this shape, stretching across 195 degrees of longitude, are over 44 million square kilometres, or 30 per cent of the earth's land area, and 4.4 billion people, or 60 per cent of the world's population. Incredibly, this continent has been sidelined in the flow of history, its dynamics determined by states on other continents for the past two centuries. No longer. This massive terrain, its scale beyond terrestrial comprehension, will henceforth be the gravitational centre of world affairs. And its unique footprint of landforms and waterscapes will set the logic of Asia's strategic dynamics and, beyond it, the world's.

Asia's geographic forms are key to understanding its security dynamics, past and future. The most defining feature of Asia's strategic geography is a formidable chain of mountains, stretching almost unbroken between the Bosporus and the South China Sea. Moving west to east, it begins with the Taurus Mountains in Asia Minor, through the Elburz and Zagros ranges in the southern Caucasus to the Hindu Kush and the Himalayas, 'a fractured rock wall, four miles high and 200 miles across',[14] still growing vertically by about 6 centimetres each year. From the eastern Himalayas, continental Southeast Asia becomes a washboard of roughly parallel mountain ranges mostly running north to south. The effect of this formidable chain of mountains stretching along Asia's southern coast has been to divide the continent into two separate strategic systems, which only occasionally in history have affected each other. Asia's northern tier comprises the majority of the continent's 44 million square kilometres: a vast area of open plains, steppes and tundra, sporadically intersected by meandering rivers and jutting mountain ranges. Its history has been written by nomadic herders and fierce mounted warrior tribes – and by two continental, paranoid empires seeking security from them. Asia's southern tier is a littoral zone, its people crowded along its coastlines by mountain ramparts, and in the case of Arabia and the subcontinent, arid desert plateaus inland. With so little land to ply, its peoples have gravitated to the ocean, and here they have inhabited and benefited from the long archipelagos of islands that bejewel Asia's southern and eastern coasts – a feature shared by no other continent on earth. They have also been blessed by another consequence of Asia's particular geography, the regular cycle of monsoon winds and rains.

In strategic terms, Asia's northern tier is a realm in which both power and vulnerability are dispersed across millions of square kilometres of rolling steppes. Asia's southern tier concentrates both power and vulnerability along crowded coastlines and waterways. The southern tier's littoral geography binds maritime and terrestrial strategy together in an unbreakable embrace. In the memorable words of French maritime strategist Raoul Castex, 'the land exercises power over the sea as if the continents overflowed the oceans as oil spreads on water'.[15] The societies of Asia's southern tier would argue that the sea exercises reciprocal strategic influence on the land: while they focused on their land frontiers, they remained oblivious to the most profound and consequential domination they ever faced – from their long coastlines across which came European colonisers, first plying trade, then conquest.

The Southern Tier

Asia's southern tier is a narrow littoral realm stretching from the Persian Gulf in the west, around the continent's southern and eastern coastlines to the Korean Peninsula and the Japanese islands in the continent's northeast corner. The southern tier comprises the continent's southern and eastern littorals and peninsulas, as well as the long island chains that begin with the Kurils in its far northeastern corner and run south through Japan, the Ryukyus, Taiwan, the Philippines and the Indonesian archipelago, before swinging west through the Andamans, Sri Lanka and the Maldives. Over three-quarters of Asia's population lives in its southern tier littorals, peninsulas and islands, within 200 kilometres of the coast.[16] In this terrestrial–maritime zone are more than 80 per cent of the continent's major cities, most of its vital infrastructure and the majority of its centres of industry, trade and military power. The age of colonisation, bringing advances in flood control and drainage technologies, led to the huge expansion of Asia's trading ports, which have continued to grow exponentially. Asia's industrialisation, beginning in the islands and peninsulas of the continent's northeast before spreading to its southeast, was concentrated in its littoral zones also, often close to great trading ports. This trend continued as industrialisation moved to the Asian continent proper. Today, over 70 per cent of China's industrial capacity is situated in its coastal provinces, up from 68.3 per cent in 2005 and 62 per cent in 1987.[17]

Asia's southern tier is a single strategic realm, bound together by the common opportunities and anxieties of societies that look out to the ocean for their vital commercial flows and which are aware that threats can also come from the ocean. An ocean orientation is a great boon to a society's prosperity; over 90 per cent of all global trade, measured by weight and volume, or 80 per cent measured by value, is carried on the world's maritime highways.[18] Before the financial crisis of 2008, global maritime traffic was growing faster than global productivity. This was even more pronounced in Asia. For the decade before the crisis, Asia's maritime trade with Europe increased by an average of 20 per cent per year. The oceans provide maritime trading states with flexibility and options to maximise profits and access the full range of what is produced by a great variety of other economies; these are huge commercial advantages that landlocked states can only dream of.

But while the ocean is a source of prosperity, it can also be a source of danger. A state's coasts are potential front lines in a conflict – long front lines offer multiple avenues of attack, beyond any state's capacities to defend them comprehensively. The world's oceans are host to the perpetual projection of military power. Even when not at war, heavily armed navies are at sea, visiting foreign ports, patrolling trade routes and engaging in seemingly innocuous 'picture-building' aimed, according to naval strategist Geoffrey Till,

> at accumulating data on the geographic characteristics of littoral areas of interest, on monitoring the political situation, and on assessing the strengths and weaknesses of other military forces... To a surprising extent this is a one-way process in which navies gain much more information than they give away.[19]

For societies whose populations, vital cities, core infrastructure and main industrial capacities are clustered along their coastlines, the promise and menace of the sea are inseparable. In an era when their neighbours were poor and focused on their internal fragility, the menace of the sea could be discounted. But in an era of rising prosperity and deepening rivalry, none of Asia's southern-tier states can afford to ignore the vulnerabilities of their coasts.

Two interlinked trends keep security planners in Asia awake at night. The first is that maritime weapons systems tend to offer rising powers a much greater potential bang for each buck spent on them. In the words of Geoffrey Till, 'maritime forces offer unimpeded access, mobility (400 miles a day compared with 30 for land forces), firepower and flexibility'.[20] Certain maritime weapons systems, such as submarines and anti-ship missiles, offer smaller countries the best chance to close the capability gap with larger powers, particularly in their capacity to deter or complicate other navies' ability to operate close to their coastlines. The other great capability equaliser is distance: the further an aggressor's forces are from home, and the closer the defender's are to its own territory, the more the advantage tips towards the defender. And navies tend to be more cost-effective and enduring: the costs of military aircraft have been rising at three times the rate of naval costs for the past three decades.[21] No southern-tier state can afford to ignore the purchase of maritime weapons systems by even the most innocuous of its neighbours.

The second trend concerns naval strategy. In Till's words, there has been a steady shift among the world's navies from deploying power *at* sea towards deploying power *from* the sea.[22] In both equipment and doctrine, the navies of the major powers are moving towards expeditionary capabilities: the capacity to project coercive force from the sea onto the land. This can be in the form of sea-based air power, ship- or submarine-launched cruise missiles, or the landing of amphibious forces. Many of these capabilities have been developed under the guise of building capacity for collaborative humanitarian and disaster relief; both India and China have demonstrated the capacity to extract theirs and their neighbours' citizens from crises in the Middle East in the past decade.[23] But few of Asia's security planners would harbour illusions that these capabilities cannot be used just as effectively for coercive ends: two decades of almost constant war in the Persian Gulf have demonstrated how devastating power from the sea can be. The only effective response for the southern-tier states, great and small alike, is to invest in the capabilities for what naval strategists call 'sea denial': the ability to deter or complicate an adversary's capacity to operate in maritime areas from which it can project power.[24] And the best weapons for sea denial are also the most cost-effective: submarines, missiles and advanced surveillance systems.

A third consideration adds fuel to Asia's maritime arms race. Asia's rising powers, no less than the superpowers during the Cold War, are similarly constrained in their ability to fight openly due to fears of economic damage and nuclear escalation. As Asia's subterranean structure of force shifts, southern-tier states have begun to experience

and anticipate new forms of coercion or non-coercive influence –
in the South and East China seas, along the Sino-Indian border, at
the line of control in Kashmir – and have begun to rehearse ways of
responding decisively but not dangerously. One possibility offered by
the southern tier's geography is what Cold War strategists called 'horizontal escalation', described by historian John Lewis Gaddis in the
following way:

> Symmetrical response [or vertical escalation] simply means
> reacting to threats to the balance of power at the same loca-
> tion, time and level of the original provocation. Asymmetrical
> response [or horizontal escalation] involves shifting the loca-
> tion or nature of one's reaction onto terrain better suited to the
> application of one's strength against the adversary's weakness.[25]

Asia's southern-tier geography, and the deepening dependence
of its states on seaborne resources, energy and market access, offers
considerable scope for the application of horizontal escalation. A
major worry for Australia and the states of Southeast Asia is that
if China gains sovereign control over the South China Sea, it could
threaten access to their important markets in Northeast Asia. Indian
strategic planners are aware that they can counter Chinese coercion
over their common border by threatening China's energy supplies
as they sail through the Indian Ocean. Pakistan's presumably have
the same thoughts about responding to India's pressure across their
mutual border. Southeast Asia's maritime states could exercise similar options in and around the Malacca Straits.

Given these trends and imperatives, it is unsurprising that
Asia's weapons acquisition statistics show a sustained build-up in
southern-tier states' maritime capabilities. In 2012, the Stockholm
International Peace Research Institute (SIPRI) reported that the
period from 2007 to 2011 saw a 200 per cent higher volume of arms

transfers into Southeast Asia than there had been between 2002 and 2006. This volume of imports was the highest since the end of the Vietnam War. Naval weapons formed the bulk of the purchases, with ships and maritime weapons accounting for 52 per cent of the total and another 37 per cent for weapons with a possible maritime role. SIPRI reports that a similar level and profile is evident in weapons acquisition intentions also.[26]

Asia has become a great arms bazaar, its states making the most of the cutthroat competition among weapons producers to procure the most effective weapons systems their money can buy. The effect of the combination of growing paranoia about seaborne threats, highly effective and affordable maritime weapons systems and the closing of military capability gaps through weapons, sea denial and distance has been to fundamentally shift the basis for strategic stability in Asia's southern tier. For 200 years, the predominant strategic order in Asia's southern tier has been one of dominance by between one and three navies, exercising what naval strategists call 'sea command'. Sea command means that a navy is so dominant it can dictate the terms of use of a given stretch of ocean: it can use it as it sees fit, while either preventing others or placing conditions on how and when they use it.[27] Following the Napoleonic Wars, this was the status Britain's Royal Navy enjoyed in the Indian Ocean; in the Pacific from the early twentieth century, it shared sea command with the navies of the United States and imperial Japan. After the end of the Second World War, the United States Navy emerged dominant in both the Pacific and Indian oceans. America used this dominance to impress its vision of world order on all inhabitants and users of Asia's Pacific and Indian ocean coasts: free trade and open access to vital markets and strategic resources, and the ability to project power onto the southern-tier littoral to prevent the rise of a power that could dominate Asia.[28]

Thanks to a cascade of maritime weapons purchases along Asia's southern tier, American sea command is crumbling. Asia's subterranean structure of force is shifting decisively, driven not by a single dominant challenge to American supremacy but as the result of linked regional dynamics. And as the latent structure of force is shifting, new possibilities and imperatives to challenge and defend existing rules and understandings are going live. The only direct challenge to the US Navy's sea command comes from the People's Republic of China.[29] Beijing has long been alarmed by the US Navy's ability to sail along its coastlines, picture-building under the cover of the doctrine of freedom of navigation, a doctrine underpinned by decades of American command of the sea. In response, China has been investing intensively in weapons of sea denial. Its current inventory of submarines is estimated at seventy, of which all but four are thought to be attack submarines. It launched an aircraft carrier, the *Liaoning*, in October 2012, and is widely suspected to be building another. But the weapon that has the Pentagon abuzz is the innocuously named Dong Feng 21D, a land-based ballistic missile which defence analysts have dubbed China's ship-killer. This high-hypersonic missile, able to be guided in flight, with a range of 1450 kilometres, is capable of carrying sufficient firepower to take out an aircraft carrier and is thought to be near-impossible to defend against. Enabled by new satellite capabilities and a nascent over-the-horizon radar system, the DF-21D has substantially increased the risks for American naval assets operating in the western Pacific.[30]

In the Indian Ocean, India is laying in similar weapons systems. Although it is as uncomfortable as Beijing about the ability of rival navies to engage in picture-building close to its coasts under cover of freedom of navigation, New Delhi is more strongly motivated by China's growing naval capabilities. While the two Asian giants continue to square off over their land borders, Indian strategists believe Beijing is preparing to project power into the Indian Ocean once it has dealt with American power in the Pacific. Of particular concern are Chinese infrastructure plans: roads, railways, pipelines and ports down to the shores of the Indian Ocean in Myanmar, Sri Lanka and Pakistan, which could become footholds for a substantial Chinese naval presence in the Indian Ocean.[31] So India too has an aircraft carrier and wants two; its fleet of attack submarines is growing through both purchase and indigenous manufacture; and its missile and surveillance systems are benefiting from strong injections of resources and political attention.

In between, along Asia's southern tier, smaller countries are developing sea denial capabilities, though on a more limited scale. Japan has enhanced its underwater surveillance systems in response to the constant intrusion by Chinese submarines into its territorial waters.[32] To complement its existing fleet of highly capable submarines, Japan has recently launched the first of two Izumo-class helicopter carriers, the largest of their type in the world. It has acquired the American-produced Aegis Combat System, along with South Korea and Australia, allowing powerful satellite-based tracking and targeting of missile systems. Japan, South Korea, Singapore, Indonesia, Australia and Pakistan have all embarked on programs to upgrade, enlarge and enhance the capabilities of their submarine fleets, while Malaysia and Vietnam have begun to acquire submarine capabilities they previously didn't possess.

Asia's narrow seas are becoming crowded with increasingly effective military hardware. The tangle of risks grows ever tighter as the chance of accident and confrontation rises with the number of submarines, ships and surveillance aircraft.[33] In this cauldron of rivalries, suspicions and new capabilities, the era of unquestioned American sea command has come to an end. While most of Asia's maritime powers are allies, partners or tacitly aligned with the United States – and Washington harbours dreams of a 'thousand-ship navy', a broad coalition of like-minded countries upholding the maritime order that used to be guaranteed by the US Navy alone[34] – Asia's rivalries and suspicions are too intense to allow such a rational outcome.

Asia's southern tier is evolving towards a system of mutual, multiple and interlocking sea denial, in which none can dictate the terms of use of Asia's waterways but most can raise the risks of others' use of them. After a long period of commanded oceans, Asia is reverting to what the great naval strategist Sir Julian Corbett described as the natural state of maritime affairs: 'the most common situation in naval war is that neither side has command; the normal position is not a commanded sea but an uncommanded sea'.[35]

Bays and Peninsulas

Afonso de Albuquerque's attack on Melaka in August 1511 was a desperate gamble by a man down on his luck. He had been despatched to the Indian Ocean in 1506 at the head of a fleet of sixteen ships, having outlined to King Manuel I a strategy for building a Portuguese empire in the east. Despite early conquests in the Persian Gulf, however, his zeal and abrasive leadership led his men to revolt and sail to India, leaving him with two ships and a handful of followers. Albuquerque followed, arriving at Cannanore on the Malabar Coast in 1508, where he proclaimed himself governor, prompting Dom Francisco de Almeida, the serving governor, to throw him in prison. Eventually Albuquerque was freed and installed to the governorship, with his impetuosity and tendency to exceed his authority undiminished. He realised that his chances of unchallenged command of the Portuguese empire of the east lay in wresting Indian Ocean trade from Muslim traders, writing in his diary, 'by taking Melaka, we would close the Straits so that never again would the Moslems be able to bring their spices by this route ... I am very sure that, if this Melaka trade is taken out of their hands, Cairo and Mecca will be completely lost'.[36] Defying orders and the protest of the Portuguese military commander in India, Albuquerque sailed for Melaka with a force of 1000 men on eighteen ships. His gamble worked: by taking Melaka the Portuguese could seal off the Indian Ocean from the Pacific trade routes, just as their control of Muscat could seal it from the Mediterranean. The Indian Ocean became a Portuguese lake, and Albuquerque gained command of the centralised administration of the Portuguese east.

Five hundred years later, dreams of establishing exclusive dominion over the ungovernable tides around Asia's coasts burn as brightly as they did in Albuquerque's imagination – and are fuelled by similar preoccupations: fear and greed. The interests of Asia's rising powers have been drawn seaward as their expectations of influence have assumed ever-more defined spatial dimensions. There is a power-security paradox at work in today's Asia: as states become more powerful, the more vulnerable they feel; the more capable they become, the less acceptable are the perceived obstacles to their rise. As their rivals and neighbours become more capable in maritime weapons systems, the urge to ward off all comers from their vulnerable coastlines becomes more insistent. But the spreading reach of these weapons systems means that any margin of sea denial never seems quite enough, and the dream of sea command, at least over limited and defined bodies of water, becomes a siren song in the imaginations of Asia's military strategists and political leaders.

The peculiarities of Asia's coastal geography are beginning to concentrate maritime competition around several partially enclosed bodies of water. Asia's foremost rising power, China, gazes seaward and sees its access to the Pacific and beyond encumbered by a rampart of islands, most of which are controlled by antagonistic regimes and allies of its great rival, the United States. Chinese strategists call this the 'first island chain', stretching from the Japanese islands through the Ryukyus, Taiwan, the Philippines and into Indonesia, and believe that this quirk of Asia's geography and postwar geopolitics hems in China's growing power.[37] The shallow waters of the South and East China seas, within the first island chain, are intensively surveilled from the air and on and below the water by the United States and its allies, utilising the seemingly innocuous advantages of overlapping territorial waters, freedom of navigation and oceanographic research.

Further to the west lie another two partially enclosed bodies of water subject to rising competition. Tucked between the Malay Peninsula and the subcontinent, the Bay of Bengal's coasts offer prime access to the lucrative trade routes of the Indian Ocean. But where other states see port and trade opportunities, India sees possible footholds for rivals. New Delhi is just as sensitive about naval picture-building in the Bay of Bengal as Beijing is about such activities in the South and East China seas. To the west of the subcontinent is the Arabian Sea, home to two of the world's most strategically crucial maritime passages: the oil-rich Persian Gulf and the Red Sea – Suez Canal gateway from the Indian Ocean to the Mediterranean. Thanks to a quarter century of almost constant war in Mesopotamia, the Arabian Sea is heavily dominated by the United States and its allies, but the growing dependence of Asia's rising powers on the energy produced in the Gulf suggests that the currents of strategic rivalry could soon begin to flow into its waters.

Until now, western strategists have spent a great deal of time discussing the vulnerability of maritime chokepoints around the Asian coastline: the Malacca and Sunda straits, the southern pass around the subcontinent, the Strait of Hormuz in the Gulf and the Bab el-Mandeb Strait in the Red Sea.[38] There is little doubt that these chokepoints, if closed to trade, could be highly disruptive. What is less certain is whether they could be closed for long enough to be strategically significant. Any power closing off such a busy trade chokepoint would, at some stage, face the resistance of others dependent on the free flow of shipping, and even if it were able to hold off those others, all chokepoints can ultimately be circumvented by sailing around longer routes.

There are signs that the imaginations of Asia's strategists are being drawn towards much grander designs. The great strategist of Britain's imperial wars, Colonel CE Calwell, pointed out over a century ago the great advantages that flowed to a maritime power that could establish control over bays and inlets:

> As, in time of war, the frontier of that nation which enjoys the maritime control is the coast line of the enemy, it follows that when the coast line takes the shape of a giant gulf or bay, the army of the power dominating the sea can strike either to the left hand or to the right, while the adversary is compelled to divide his forces.[39]

The geography of bays interacts with power and the strategic imagination of rising powers in peculiar ways. Bays are enclosed bodies of water that engage the territorial imagination – one can imagine commanding a bay much more easily than one can imagine commanding a sea or an ocean. The enclosed waters of a bay concentrate maritime competition; the realities of one side's navy dominating its waters, or the navies of others contesting that domination, are much starker and more obvious than on the open ocean. Rather than threatening to close off chokepoints, the command of a bay promises a much more enduring form of power, particularly if the commanding state can set and enforce rules governing others' use of those waters.

Asia's three great bays – the Arabian Sea, the Bay of Bengal and the South China Sea – are the sites of growing competition and rivalry among Asia's maritime powers. All three are integral to Asia's crucial flow of hydrocarbons; all three provide ingress and egress to the crucial maritime passages and chokepoints of the Indian and Pacific oceans; and all three are bordered by slightly different collections of ambitious great powers and insecure smaller states. Each of Asia's great bays engages historical imaginations also; historian Janet Abu-Lughod has shown that before the imperial age, the Arabian Sea, the Bay of Bengal and the South China Sea each had its own distinctive monsoon rhythm and each was plied by different traders who trans-shipped their goods at key ports such as Melaka for others to take onwards.[40] So, just as China has a strong sense of historical ownership of the South China Sea, India feels similarly towards the Bay of Bengal and the Arabian Sea. Unsurprisingly, these claims of ownership are disputed and resented by other states that overlook these bodies of water.

History aside, the South China Sea presents more immediate strategic imperatives for Beijing. Within the waters between the Philippine archipelago and the Asian coastline, the waters of the first island chain broaden and deepen, and the Luzon Strait offers broad egress from the southern coast of China to the Pacific in a way that the narrow straits of the first island chain further north do not. Almost all of China's hydrocarbon imports and the majority of its seaborne trade sail through the South China Sea, making that body of water and its points of ingress and egress a key vulnerability of a China increasingly dependent on overseas trade and energy flows. Motivated by both the advantages and vulnerabilities of the South China Sea, Beijing has built a huge naval base with underground submarine pens at Sanya on Hainan Island, which dominates the northern reaches of the South China Sea.[41] As the Sanya base has become operational, China has, not surprisingly, become increasingly sensitive about oceanographic surveillance being conducted in the South China Sea by the United States and its allies. Aside from its many scientific virtues, oceanographic research is essential for preparing a navy for submarine tracking and warfare.

As early as the 1970s, Beijing had claimed most of the South China Sea as its territorial waters, with the National People's Congress going as far as writing these claims into China's domestic law in 1992. These claims have been disputed by the Philippines, Vietnam, Malaysia and Brunei at points where their own territorial waters overlap with the Chinese claims. Indonesia is increasingly worried about the overlap of China's claims with the waters around its own oil-rich Natuna Island territory. Other states with non-territorial interests in the South China Sea – including the United States, Japan, India and Australia – have asserted that much of China's claim covers international waters that should remain subject to a regime of freedom of navigation.[42] Beijing rejects calls for arbitration or the possibility of regional organisations finding a solution. Chinese naval and coastguard vessels continue to challenge ships transiting the South China Sea, while Chinese bases are under construction in the Spratly and Paracel island groups, both claimed by other countries. Armed clashes have occurred between Chinese forces and Vietnamese and Philippine naval forces.

The Bay of Bengal has long been a focus of ambition and anxiety for India. America's intimidating positioning of the aircraft carrier group USS *Enterprise* in the Bay of Bengal during India's 1971 war with Pakistan ranks almost as highly as defeat in the 1962 Sino-Indian border war in the memory of defence officials in New Delhi. India's first prime minister, Jawaharlal Nehru, was the first to suggest America's Monroe Doctrine as a model for India's ambition to be able to exclude hostile interests from the Indian Ocean, an ambition that is strongly held by India's defence elites half a century later.[43] Indian maritime doctrine envisages the ability to close off the entry and exit points to the Indian Ocean and the capacity to exercise sea command in a series of concentric rings spreading south from the subcontinent into the Indian Ocean. India's military doctrine has a diplomatic counterpart: a permanent offer of assistance, coupled with clear discouragement of assistance from other countries, should any of its Indian Ocean neighbours require help. New Delhi's interventions in Bangladesh after 1971, Sri Lanka from 1983 to 1990 and the Maldives in 1988, and its trade pressure on Nepal in 1989–90 show how seriously India takes this doctrine.

Geography offers India several advantages in the Bay of Bengal. It has major naval and air bases at Visakhapatnam on the western coast of the bay, as well as at Port Blair in the Andaman Island chain in the bay's eastern waters. India's Andaman and Nicobar islands form a screen across the westward approaches to the Strait of Malacca. Unlike China, India has been determined to resolve its territorial disputes with Bangladesh and Myanmar in the Bay of Bengal, and to coax them into joint naval patrols and exercises. But neither country, nor Sri Lanka, seems willing to blithely acquiesce to Indian command of the bay.[44] All three of India's smaller neighbours have expressed support for China's proposal for a 'maritime silk road' through the Indian Ocean, and Chinese investment and expertise has been welcomed for the building of ports at Kyauk Phyu in Myanmar, Chittagong in Bangladesh and Hambantota in Sri Lanka.

To the west of the subcontinent, the Arabian Sea appears less a bay of competition than a haven for pirates and a platform for projecting American power into the various Gulf conflicts. But there are signs that it too could become more heavily contested over time. The importance of the Arabian Sea lies in its access to the Persian Gulf and the Red Sea and therefore to the large volumes of commercial and energy shipping that traverse these waters. The strategic geography of the Gulf in particular shapes the broader strategic dynamics of the Arabian Sea. Four characteristics of the Gulf shape its essential security dynamics. First, its narrowness makes it highly vulnerable to sustained blockage, which in turn makes land access to its lower reaches, bypassing its chokepoints, highly desirable. Second, its shallowness and the span of the region's vast hydrocarbon reservoirs under political boundaries make the Gulf home to an intense thicket of territorial disputes. Third, the severe imbalances between the wealth and size of the Gulf states – most are small and hugely wealthy but threatened by the region's one giant, Shiite Iran – make the region heavily dependent on imported military power and security. Fourth, the ethnic and religious diversity, autocratic political structures and petro-state fragilities of the Gulf states act as a magnet for transnational and external meddling, constantly threatening to draw external security providers into the domestic instabilities of the region.[45]

Taken together, these four factors make certain developments in the Gulf more likely. The combination of internal fragility, transnational influences, external meddling and territorial rivalries makes dissension among the Gulf states a strong possibility. Currently, the collective fear of Iran encourages a certain solidarity among the Gulf's Sunni states, but this could unravel quickly – especially if violent domestic change brings to power religious fundamentalists in one or more of the Gulf's Sunni states.[46] Another distinct possibility is that the will of the United States to be the sole security provider to the Gulf states will ebb. America faces a strong challenge to its naval supremacy in Asia's eastern waters; notwithstanding Washington's 'rebalance' towards the Pacific, it is hard to see how a shrinking US Navy can maintain the intensity of its operations in West Asia while meeting the challenge to its pre-eminence in the Pacific at the same time. These two developments will almost certainly lead to a third: oil-rich Gulf states will begin looking to other security providers and will likely find willing partners among Asia's energy-hungry rising powers.[47] Something of a dress rehearsal for this is already taking place in the Gulf of Aden, where Japan, China, South Korea, India and Pakistan are contributing ships alongside those of NATO nations to a collective anti-piracy operation. These Asian powers' warships are hardly necessary in the Gulf of Aden; the combined forces of NATO and the Gulf states are more than a match for a few Somali pirates. Asia's navies are there to show their capabilities and to familiarise themselves with the political and strategic geography of the Arabian Sea.

The tempo of competition is already rising. China has invested heavily in building a deepwater port at Gwadar on the Pakistan coast, just outside the mouth of the Gulf, intending to link to it with roads, rail and pipelines stretching to China's western provinces. India has countered by investing in the port of Chabahar on the Iranian coast, just further into the Gulf, and proposing a north–south transport corridor to Afghanistan and Central Asia.

The rivalrous dynamics of Asia's southern tier will concentrate not just in its three great bays, but also along the peninsulas that divide and frame these bays. CE Calwell drew attention to the military significance of peninsulas over a century ago. Peninsulas, he argued, by definition lack strategic depth; they are the very opposite of a land-based salient into enemy territory:

> The salient land frontier does not necessarily place troops within the salient at a strategical disadvantage; because they may be in a position to strike; and there are two different directions in which they can strike. But an army in a salient girt by the sea cannot from the nature of the case strike if the enemy has command of the sea.[48]

Peninsular geography interacts with power and the strategic imagination in distinctive ways: it constrains, concentrates, funnels and bundles power. Peninsular states have no strategic depth they can retreat into if attacked from the sea; an enemy that gains a foothold at any point on the peninsula gains a base from which to launch attacks on the remainder. Strategic shifts in one part of a peninsula are likely to cascade to its other parts. Peninsulas tend to be strategically stable if dominated by a single set of strategic interests, but once a contrary strategic interest gains a hold, they become extremely unstable. Japan's lightning campaign down the Pacific archipelago and the Malay Peninsula during the Second World War shows how vulnerable the remainder of a peninsula becomes once a hostile force gains a foothold; the Allied island-hopping campaign to push Japan back shows how difficult it is to draw and hold a defensive position on a peninsula.[49]

Rivalries around Asia's three great peninsulas will shape strategic competition for its three great bays; with a wink to Mackinder it might be said that the 'bays hold the key to the peninsulas, while the peninsulas hold the key to the bays'. The three strategically significant peninsulas of Asia's southern tier are the West Pacific Peninsula, the archipelago of islands stretching from Japan in the north through Taiwan and the Philippines, or what Chinese strategists call the first island chain; the Indo-Pacific Peninsula, running from Thailand through Malaysia and Indonesia to Australia; and the South Asian Peninsula, commonly called the subcontinent.

The West Pacific and South Asian peninsulas each hold the key to China's and India's freedom to engage fully in the southern tier's growing rivalry. Each are held in full or part by rival entities; each peninsula contains as separate countries territories that are integral to India's and China's historic sense of wholeness, and these alienated territories provide strategic footholds for major rivals. For China, Taiwan represents the key to gaining control of the West Pacific Peninsula. Beijing has always claimed Taiwan as a renegade province, insisting that all countries with which it has relations must acknowledge this also. If Beijing is able to gain actual control over the island, Chinese forces on Taiwan would be uncomfortably close to Japanese defences over the Ryukyu Islands, which include the American base on Okinawa, and, while further away, the northern Philippines would be in striking distance. In addition to turning Japan's southern maritime flank and threatening the largest American base in Asia, a Chinese Taiwan would, in the words of naval strategists James

Holmes and Toshi Yoshihara, function as 'a guard tower in an off-shore Great Wall', allowing China to project force deep into the South China Sea and out into the mid-Pacific, forming a defensive perimeter of unsinkable island bases screening China's mainland from the power of maritime rivals.[50] But while Taiwan and the rest of the West Pacific Peninsula remain in the hands of renegades, rivals and American allies, it remains the foremost preoccupation of Chinese strategists, preventing Beijing from bringing its full power to bear on the competition for Asia's three bays.

Likewise, India feels vulnerable to rivals or possible rivals on the South Asian Peninsula. Indian strategists regard the entire subcontinent as a single strategic entity and believe its subdivision to create the states of Pakistan, Bangladesh and Nepal is a source of distraction and weakness. Nearly seventy years of almost constant tension and repeated wars with Pakistan have dragged India's attention inwards to its borders on the subcontinent, not to mention dragging a proudly non-aligned nation into the jealousies of the Cold War. It has become almost an obsession among Indian strategists that the subdivisions of the subcontinent allow its other rivals such as China to gain a foothold in the South Asian Peninsula, building Pakistan's capabilities in order to tie down Indian power. Insecurities over its borders with Pakistan and China have limited New Delhi's ability to build maritime capabilities and project power beyond the subcontinent. A growing body of elite opinion in New Delhi believes that India must resolve tensions with Pakistan, and integrate economically with all of its neighbours in South Asia, to free itself to meet rising challenges on its northeast and maritime frontiers.[51]

The Indo-Pacific Peninsula is crucial because it is a land and island barrier between the Indian Ocean and the Pacific Ocean. When Chinese strategists look southward, they worry about China's 'Malacca dilemma' – the prospect that hostile forces could close off the Malacca, Sunda and Lombok straits through the Indo-Pacific

Peninsula, thus choking off trade and energy flows to China.[52] Japan, Korea, Taiwan, Vietnam and the Philippines all face the same danger. Beijing's frenetic building of infrastructure from its southern provinces through Myanmar to the Bay of Bengal, and its western provinces through Pakistan to the Arabian Sea, is testament to the formidable barrier it sees in the Indo-Pacific Peninsula. When Indian strategists look eastwards, they see the Indo-Pacific Peninsula as a door that could be used to keep hostile interests out of the Indian Ocean. Needless to say, were China to gain significant influence or allies among the states of the Indo-Pacific Peninsula, it would allay its Malacca dilemma to a great extent and allow Beijing to project power effectively both into the Southern Pacific Ocean and the Indian Ocean. On the other hand, were any of China's rivals to gain such a foothold on the peninsula, it would turn China's Malacca dilemma into a constant Malacca threat.

Currently, the Indo-Pacific Peninsula is shared among a collection of smaller and middle powers partnered or allied with the United States but with strong commercial and institutional relations with each of Asia's major powers. For almost half a century they have shared a commitment to solidarity and the equidistant engagement with all regional powers, lest the prospect of advantage for one lead to accelerating and destructive rivalry among all in the region. It is a formula that has served them well, though during times of reduced rivalry among the powers.[53] An enterprising great power could make great use of the latent rivalries among some of the peninsula's states or of the periodic domestic political instability in some of them. Imperial Japan exploited tension between Thailand and then-Indochina over border demarcations as a pretext to mediate and then set up a sphere of influence before it had even fired a shot in its push down the Malay Peninsula. Meanwhile, western and ASEAN diplomats worry that China's economic influence has made considerable headway in drawing small, impoverished states such as Cambodia and Laos into a Chinese sphere of influence in Southeast Asia.

As the shifting tides of wealth and power alter the structure of force underlying Asia's southern tier, the lines of what can be credibly challenged and what will be safely enforced are moving also. The end of unquestioned American sea command provides avenues for the paranoid ambitions of Asia's rising powers to contemplate their own zones of command and supremacy. But China and India must first summon the will and art to break out of their own individual peninsular dilemmas, while their rivals must weigh up the limits and possibilities of their efforts to keep these two powers tied down by these peninsulas. Meanwhile, the southern tier's smaller states ponder what fate such rivalry holds for them, contributing to the fluidity of the strategic dynamics by investing in their own weapons systems and security alignments. And as urgent as these rivalries seem, no southern-tier state wants to see the lucrative economic linkages among them disrupted by unrestrained power competition.

The Northern Tier

In the spring of 1652, a contingent of Manchu troops sent by China's Qing Dynasty attacked a garrison of Russian Cossacks near the village of Wu-cha-la in the Amur River valley in northern Manchuria. They had been dispatched in response to the pleas of the local Daur tribes, who were vassals of the Qing Court but had been subject to brutal Cossack raids led by the Russian adventurer Erofei Pavlovich Khabarov. For the previous two years, armed with muskets and cannon, Khabarov and his Cossacks staged brutal raids along the Amur River, intoxicated by the riches of its grain fields and convinced that personal fortune and the glory of the Russian Empire would be boosted if the local people became vassals to Moscow. The Qing troops were commanded by an experienced general, Hai-Tze, and with a sustained bombardment quickly gained the upper hand against the Cossacks. But Hai-Tze had been ordered to intimidate and drive off the Cossacks, not to destroy them. He issued orders to his troops to avoid killing the enemy, allowing Khabarov to rally his troops. The Cossacks counter-attacked and drove off the Qing force, killing 676 Manchus to only ten Russian dead.[54]

This was the moment when the strategic logic of the geography of Asia's northern tier became fully manifest. Barricaded from the Indian Ocean by the great ramparts of Asia's east–west mountain chain, and bounded to the north by the Arctic, the northern tier is the earth's greatest plain. Like a giant tablecloth thrown onto the planet's surface, despite the occasional wrinkle of the Tian Shan or Pamir mountains and scattered rips and spills of meandering rivers and lakes, the northern tier is, for the most part, a vast expanse of flat basins, plains and steppes, of forests, grasslands, deserts and tundra stretching seemingly endlessly in every direction. On this strategic tabula rasa there are no barriers formidable enough to inhibit, shape or divide the manifestations of human fear and aggression. This landscape bred fierce nomad warrior tribes, hardened by constant existential warfare, that coalesced early in the second millennium and spilled across the northern tier in all directions, conquering the largest land empire the world has ever seen. The trauma of the Mongol onslaught has never left two of the peoples it conquered, each clustered around a river system on the eastern and western boundaries of the northern tier. Both the Chinese, who settled around the Yangtze River and Yellow River basins, and the Russians between the Dnieper and Volga rivers, had always faced raids from fierce Central Asian tribes, but nothing could have prepared them for the brutality of the Mongol assault – or cause them to forget their helplessness against it. 'The appearance in the winter of 1236–7 of Mongol horsemen deep in the forest zone,' writes historian Richard Pipes, 'caused a shock that has never been quite erased from the collective consciousness of the Russian people.'[55] They moved, recounted a contemporary Arab observer, 'like a darkness chased by a cloud'.

The Russians and the Chinese were peoples imbued with a sense of civilisational mission, while Mongol power proved as brittle as the lives of its great khans. The two riverine peoples set about building enduring civilisations, always aware of the threat of sudden outbursts of nihilistic aggression from the anarchic tribes of the steppes. The Russians built stockades to protect their frontier towns; the Chinese began to construct a monumental wall as early as the third century BCE, under their legendary first emperor Qin Shihuangdi. But defensive orientations left surrounding warrior tribes with the strategic and tactical initiative, and slowly both empires pushed into the heart of Asia, subduing the tribes and bringing their anarchic nomadism under the rule of tsar and emperor. The empires' creeping rule was not only about defence; each also found its expanding hinterland to be a source of wealth and power.[56] Before the modern age, Central Asia supplied the great empires of China, India and Persia with an estimated 100,000 war horses every year; later it became a source of coveted furs, then of minerals, energy, resources and cotton. Once the Chinese and Russian empires started expanding into the centre of Asia, there was nothing to stop them; an inexorable logic drew them onwards. Every expansion of their frontiers brought new, different, fiercely independent peoples within their borders, and endowed those borders with a new set of restive and covetous neighbours. It was only when the two empires met that the limit to their expansion was found, and soon they were confronted by a third empire, the British, pushing into Central Asia from the subcontinent.[57]

The quest for security through expansion only created different forms of insecurity for the Chinese and Russian empires. As their boundaries crept forward, each empire acquired new, restive domestic minorities and powerful external rivals, thereby instilling in both a permanent anxiety about domestic and external danger. Both had acquired rich hinterlands, the source of wealth and strategic depth, and nagging fears about insurrection and aggression within and across vast indefensible frontiers. The geography of the northern tier has always dispersed power and vulnerability for the two great empires that control its spaces.[58] Each worries that its rich but underpopulated hinterlands are subject to the avaricious designs of the other. Each has the option of grabbing territory from the other or fomenting the other's restive minorities into simmering rebellion. When relations between Moscow and Beijing soured in the 1920s, 1930s and 1960s, the former had little hesitation in stirring up rebellious interests in China's Xinjiang province.[59] And later, in the depths of the Sino-Soviet split, each had little hesitation in unleashing the full fury of its artillery against the other across the meandering Ussuri River.

The Soviet Union tried to address the internal fragility of the empire it inherited by designating certain territories around its southern and western borders as republics within a Moscow-controlled union. But Joseph Stalin was too cynical and acute a politician to make these boundaries reflect the Bukhara, Khiva and Kokand khanates that had succumbed to Russian rule in Central Asia in the nineteenth century. Instead, the Soviet republics were an arbitrary mix of peoples, each designed to be heavily dependent on Soviet Russia economically, politically and culturally.[60] Further north, Mongolia, which had been ruled from Beijing since the seventeenth century, became embroiled in the Russian civil war, eventually becoming an independent state aligned to Moscow in 1921. When the Soviet Union collapsed, its Central Asian republics – Kazakhstan, Kyrgyzstan, Uzbekistan, Tajikistan and Turkmenistan – joined Mongolia and Afghanistan as independent states sandwiched between the two great northern-tier empires.

History has left the northern tier divided into two continent-sized empires and a straggling landlocked archipelago of smaller states. The imperial logic of a Lord Curzon would designate the members of this archipelago as buffer states, designed to physically separate the avarice and anxieties of the two empires. Here lies the key to the strategic dynamics of the northern tier: whether Russia and China can suppress their rivalries and unease and continue to refuse to make the smaller Central Asian states the site of renewed imperial competition. Since the collapse of the Soviet Union, Beijing and Moscow have maintained a pragmatic, if wary, embrace, born of a realisation of mutual vulnerability.[61] Overt competition across Asia's northern tier would almost certainly result in the type of domestic instability that would threaten their rule over their economically crucial but underpopulated hinterlands. An accommodation in Central Asia has allowed Moscow to focus on its fractious relations with the Atlantic community and its troubled Caucasian flank; it has allowed Beijing to turn its energy towards its Pacific coast, the epicentre of its economic rise. The symbol of the Sino-Russian accommodation is the Shanghai Cooperation Organisation, a largely content-free regional body that brings together Russia, China and four of the former Soviet republics.

But there is a structural fragility in this accommodation, born of the legacy of the northern tier's strategic geography, that affects all of its states, large and small. History has left the states in Central Asia sparsely populated, reliant on extremely narrow economic bases and, apart from Mongolia, with little sense of national cohesion.[62] The smaller landlocked states feel their isolation and dependence on the two enveloping empires acutely, sporadically dreaming of corridors to the Indian Ocean including via association with their Turkic-speaking kin to the southwest. Theirs is a long tradition of balancing between Russia and China, using one as reassurance when the demands of the other become too overbearing.

The former Soviet republics have each opted for secular semi-authoritarian governments, as fearful of the threats of democratic movements and Islamist revivalism as are their counterparts in Beijing and Moscow. All are acutely aware that their domestic harmony can be destabilised at any time by the efforts of their neighbours to ensure their own domestic stability. A cocktail of authoritarianism, corruption and economic underperformance makes the states and provinces of Central Asia ripe for Islamic extremism, ethnic unrest and democratic discontent.[63]

Onto these shaky foundations, China and Russia each project their fears and ambitions. Beijing's solution to the unrest in Xinjiang is economic development; the historical materialist mind sees a logical, inevitable causality between prosperity, contentment and the recasting of primordial loyalties. Now into its third decade, China's strategy is to integrate Xinjiang economically with the rest of China, as well as to the rest of Asia.[64] The most recent manifestation of this is President Xi Jinping's commitment to building a 'New Silk Road Economic Belt' – an extensive and integrated network of commerce, investment and infrastructure – from China's inland provinces west and southwest through the Asian heartland. The integration project has been highly successful, even if the political project has not; China is now the largest trade partner of all the northern-tier states. For Beijing, economic connectivity is inseparable from political influence; it expects that its ability to work with governments to curb factors aggravating domestic stability in Xinjiang will also travel along the New Silk Road.

To Moscow, the prospect of part of its economic hinterland gravitating to the larger and more dynamic Chinese economy is disturbing. Since the Soviet collapse, Russia has attempted to maintain close relations with the former republics through a variety of means, often bordering on sphere-of-interest actions. President Putin's latest move is to unveil a Eurasian Economic Union that aims to draw the former Soviet republics into a customs union rivalling the European Union. But the trends are not positive for Russia. Already its trade with the Central Asian states is less than half that of China, by volume and value – and the trends show this discrepancy widening steadily. And history suggests that as Moscow's relations with the west start to slide towards Cold War levels of hostility, it will place ever greater emphasis on its fortunes in Central Asia.[65] Yet countries such as Uzbekistan have demonstrated a clear determination to remain aloof from too warm a Russian embrace. The combination of external rivalries, internal discontents and imperial jealousies is a potentially explosive cocktail in the heart of Asia. Despite all surface evidence of the pragmatic accommodation between Russia and China, there are deep sources of underlying fragility that could break out into open rivalry between the two empires across Asia's northern tier.

Across Asia's landforms and seascapes, steep trajectories of development and wealth are animating the fears and empowering the ambitions of most of its forty-four states. The subterranean latent structure of force that underpins all conventions and understandings is shifting most markedly in Asia. And yet it is upon the continued stability of these conventions and understandings that the ongoing development of Asia's jostling states depends most powerfully. Asia's divided strategic geography has concentrated most of the rivalry and contention in its southern tier, while a pragmatic though tenuous balance of common vulnerabilities between China and Russia keeps the northern tier's rivalries dormant.

China – the continent's most populous state, largest and most dynamic economy and most ambitious strategic actor – is also the only country that simultaneously occupies both the southern and northern tiers. Herein lies a key truth of China's future strategic potential. While other Asian countries can dabble in the tier they do not occupy – for example, India's designs in Central Asia or Russia's in the subcontinent – China is inescapably bound and shaped by the different imperatives and dynamics of Asia's two strategic tiers. It has been an age-old truism of Chinese statecraft that grappling with the demands of two restive strategic realms is beyond its capacities. When China's inner borders were at issue, it traditionally turned away from the sea, while any period of quiescence on its land borders has allowed it to fulfil its potential toward the Pacific. Now, its sense of destiny and determination as it embraces its coastal opportunities and challenges is tempered by nagging worries that, at any moment, its vulnerable internal frontiers could once again become a source of existential challenge.

These strategic vistas have played host to so much history. Even as empires, technologies and coveted commodities have swept across them, Asia's particular landforms and waterscapes have channelled and shaped the continent's strategic dynamics into recurring patterns. As wealth, dynamism and power re-congregate on this vast continent, we would be unwise to ignore the iron disciplines of its geography, the subtle shifts in its subterranean structures of violence or the familiar corridors of blood and ambition that have long been drawn across and around this pivotal continent.

6

ASIA AND THE WORLD

Why Asia? Why not Africa, with its youthful demographic profile and geology studded with mineral and energy wealth? Or Europe, with its prosperous, educated and peaceful population, its temperate climate and sophisticated governance and social infrastructures? Or the Anglosphere, responsible for the global currency, the world's lingua franca, its highest ideals of rights and limitations on power? Or the coming great powers, be they BRICS or some other combination, that will arrange the world between them? Why concentrate on the power dynamics across the continent of Asia as a meditation on what will shape the world we and our children will live in for the next century and beyond?

There are four compelling reasons why Asia and not Africa, Europe, the Anglosphere or a scattered collection of great powers will be the major shaper of the world for the foreseeable future. The first is simply *scale*. Interlinked revolutions in connectivity – of communications, technologies, industrial organisation, knowledge and culture creation – have reinserted population back into the productivity equation, delivering major advantages to poorer but stable societies. In no geographic location has this been more pronounced than on the continent of Asia. Both of the world's billion-plus societies, each encompassing one-fifth of humanity, nestle among a dozen other heavily populated countries. In their bustling cities, industrial parks and special economic zones the invisible hand of economic distribution – with some gentle guidance from Asian governments – has chosen to site an increasing proportion of global economic activity. The result: the fastest, largest and most sustained growth in income in human history, which continues to spread to countries across the continent. Economic geographers, who plot the concentration of economic activity across the earth's surface, have been tracking the centre of gravity of the global economy as it moves steadily in a southeastern direction from the point where it began the twentieth century in the middle of the North Atlantic Ocean. By the middle of the twenty-first century, they predict it will hover somewhere above the disputed border between India and China.[1]

Reason two is *muscle memory*. The sheer persistence of government in Asian societies, through cycles of expansion, decline and conquest, is a major reason for their historical glory and sustained development today. Asian societies seem to possess a governance DNA that ensures the formation and reformation of the state form over many centuries. It is no accident that in Asia the sovereign state form – a technology of governance developed in Europe – has been most successfully adopted and adapted to accommodate pre-colonial understandings of power and authority. Indeed, as state power has been tamed and bounded in Europe and its settler offshoots by democratic and legal institutions, it is in Asia where the command power of the state endures – and would be much more recognisable to Louis XIV than the workings of today's Fifth Republic in France. Long tradition has meant that Asian societies tend to invest both authority and hope in the command power of the state to deliver outcomes from development to security.[2] The state in Asia has willingly accepted this role, promising stability and prosperity in return for the confidence of its citizens – and not too great an insistence on regular changes of government or transparency in its workings. Asia's powerful states, unfettered by the need for compromise, will increasingly be determined players on the world stage.

The third reason is *pride*, a sense among Asian states of the importance of their culture and civilisation that drives an assertiveness and prickliness not displayed by most non-Asian states. The process of nation-building that followed decolonisation in Asia has led to deep investments in history and great attention being paid to periods of historical greatness. There are two contexts in which civilisational pride affects Asian states' international behaviour. The first is when their interactions with western states recall in some way the colonial domination of Asia, implying as it did the superiority of western countries in knowledge, technology, learning and organisation. The need to reassert a sense of self-worth after the experience of domination seems not to have waned much even as the ranks of those who actually experienced colonial rule become thinner and thinner.[3] The other context that awakens feelings of cultural chauvinism is when Asian states' neighbours make claims to historical greatness. A competitive cultural dynamic is deeply ingrained across Asia: as each society is determined to regain a sense of pride by investing in a sense of its historical greatness, it touches off a jealous response from its neighbours.[4] Before the arrival of European imperialism, most great kingdoms could be pre-eminent in their own semi-isolated geographic realms, but with their incorporation into a global system, the struggle for respect has and will continue to be constant and a significant driver of Asian powers' international behaviour.

The fourth and final reason is *location*. Just as proximity led European states' economic dynamism and military rivalry to spread across the continent and then burst forth from the continent to reorder the world, so the adjacency of Asian powers' dynamic development, growing power and ambition and deepening rivalries is driving a domino effect of prosperity and rivalry across the continent – and ultimately beyond. The logics of industrial integration, energy demand and investment are forging a coherent strategic and geoeconomic realm across Asia, from the Mediterranean to the Pacific. The prosperity and power of Asian states are constituting a larger and larger proportion of global balances with each passing year, and whether as security providers, or investors or commodity customers or tourists, the concentric rings of Asian states' influences will radiate ever further, becoming increasingly important influences on the fates of societies in other continents. Meanwhile, Asia's strategic geographies mean that rivalries and alignments will concentrate around particular physical features, such as bays and peninsulas, or political features, such as chains of buffer states. The contests around these features will be increasingly consequential for states across Asia, as well as for those on other continents.

Each of these is a strong reason for taking seriously Asia's impact on the world of the twenty-first century; taken together, each inflating the consequences of the other, these reasons present a compelling case. Two questions remain: how will the international relations of Asia develop in the decades ahead, and how will these continental dynamics in turn affect the world?

Continental Tectonics

There are two predominant and opposed narratives concerning the rapid enrichment and empowerment of Asia's largest societies. One is that all will be well and that, by mid-century, Asia will be a prosperous and peaceful continent; the other is that wealth and power will lead to competition and war, both hot and cold.[5] But there are strong signs that the actual consequences of rapid empowerment and enrichment in Asia will be much more complex. There are three compelling reasons why the sustained surge in wealth and power in Asia will cause turbulence, but not necessarily lead to sustained conflict.

First, the overwhelming weight of history shows that economic growth is not secular, if secular means that growth can occur without affecting a society's perceptions and beliefs. Wealth and power are two fundamental locators of a state's sense of itself in the world; those with more wealth and power invariably have a more expansive sense of their rights and prerogatives than those with less. History shows that larger societies tend to be more moralistic in their interpretations of international affairs: wealth and power require a sense of moral rectitude both to be amassed and used and to justify the actions of the wealthy and powerful. Smaller and poorer societies, of necessity, view international affairs more pragmatically and more often than not do not share powerful and wealthy states' virtuous self-perceptions. Hence sudden shifts in wealth or power cannot but alter societies' perceptions, expectations and beliefs. Asian societies' recent histories of colonialism and domination, along with the deeply hierarchic social relations and worldviews, mean that relatively sudden adjustments in wealth and power will acquire great significance when it comes to rights, prerogatives and perceptions of justice. Asia's two largest societies have a long tradition of looking at international affairs through a moralistic lens; it would be odd indeed if their sudden rise has not been interpreted in terms of virtue and prerogative. Meanwhile, the sense of self of most of their smaller but still substantial neighbours has been heightened by their growth in wealth and power, as well as by the growing pretensions of their giant neighbours.

Second, as they become more wealthy and powerful, Asian states are becoming progressively less self-sufficient. The prerogatives of economic growth, themselves compelling for governments keen to shore up their legitimacy, mean that their economies increasingly require what cannot be found within their borders – be they deep wells of low-cost energy, or millions of cashed-up customers, or high-quality low-cost component parts, or technology, or education. With each growing external dependency, the network of external commitments grows thicker and more comprehensive, and the sense that these must be carefully nurtured more compelling. Taiwan and South Korea are cases in point. Both countries have a remarkably similar economic profile, being world leaders in the manufacture of electronic component parts, particularly microprocessors and computer chips. When the government in Seoul began negotiating a trade agreement with China, the world's largest importer of these components, Taipei became worried. If South Korea gained preferential access to China's market, it would reap not only trade gains but also billions of dollars of investment as microprocessor manufacturers relocated their production to South Korea. Taipei, despite the shadow of hundreds of Chinese missiles pointing its way, began pushing for a trade agreement with China too.[6]

Third, the enrichment and empowerment of Asia's states has led to deepening rivalries among them. An enduring feature of Asia's international relations, originating in pre-colonial times and persisting to the present, has been overlapping mandalas of suspicion and mistrust. It is hard to look at the political map of Asia and find two countries next to each other that enjoy substantial trust and alignment, as one finds between the United States and Canada, or Australia and New Zealand, or among various European states. Where alignments do exist in Asia, they are more often than not generated by shared antipathy for a third country. Needless to say, any genuine black-letter alliances in Asia are with non-Asian powers such as the United States.

With Asia's growing wealth, the rivalries among Asian societies are increasingly reminiscent of genuine power competition. A 'normalisation' of Asian security is occurring. On gaining independence, most Asian states inherited colonial boundaries that included a great deal of diversity and rivalry, and many soon acquired communist insurgencies also. The result was ethnic and political instability and a consequent preoccupation with domestic security in a way that crowded out serious external security preparation or competition. Security spending in Asia has shifted decisively in favour of external security over the past decade. While few of those countries that, in the past, were preoccupied with internal security would admit that their domestic concerns have been completely resolved, the shift in favour of external security reflects intensified strategic competition in the region. Thus, despite its internal security budget being larger than its military budget, China's arms spending continues to grow strongly.[7] As a result, Asian countries on the whole are becoming more able to prosecute their own external security interests – and as ability grows, willingness follows closely. Asia is becoming a more militarised realm, with a greater number of consequential actors. The options for both rivalries and coalitions have expanded, as have the chances of conflict occurring between militaries whose capabilities exceed their doctrine or maturity.

In combination, these three trends – entitlement, interdependence and rivalry – suggest that Asia's international relations will neither be entirely peaceful nor destined for incessant warfare. In the world of the past, rapid enrichment and empowerment, and resulting entitlement and rivalry, would be resolved by a general war. Such wars – among European kingdoms for instance – would clear the international air of brooding jealousies, imagined slights and secret pacts. General wars among great powers in the past resulted in what one international relations writer has called 'strategic resets' – unambiguous understandings of which states were powerful and which had lost power, and therefore which states had the right to make the new rules and the capacity to enforce them.[8] But in twenty-first century Asia, an air-clearing war is no longer an option. The vital economic connections among Asian societies, not to mention the nuclear arsenals of some, make the prospect of war utterly self-defeating. Apart from anything else, no major Asian power has the energy self-sufficiency required to fuel a major war – since one of the first connections targeted in such a war would be energy supply lines. The same can be said for self-sufficiency in weapons systems; even though China and India are investing heavily in their weapons industries, they still have major gaps. Asia's pre-eminent power, China, for example, is still unable to make advanced jet-fighter engines.[9] Unable to give war a chance, Asia's international relations will most likely continue to be animated by unrequited rivalries.

Just as eighteenth-century Europe is an unlikely template for twenty-first century Asia, so is twentieth-century Europe. After the Second World War, rival states in Europe, fearing another destructive general war, built on their economic interdependences to forge a regional compact of mutual trust and deepening political integration. But the prospects of the states of Asia launching a project to develop their economic interdependencies into a continent-wide system of political integration are vanishingly small. The rivalries are substantial and getting larger; the mistrust is deepening. Even at the subregional level, such as in Southeast Asia, over half a century of regional association has brought no meaningful political integration or noticeably reduced intermural mistrust. In recent years, two ASEAN members, Thailand and Cambodia, have exchanged fire in a dispute over a temple located on their border, while the territorial dispute between the Philippines and Malaysia has been aggravated by the arbitrary actions of a self-appointed sultan. Meanwhile, Indonesia, the region's erstwhile *primus inter pares*, continues to drag its feet over meaningful regional economic integration out of fear that this will lead to its own economic *dis*integration.

Without recourse to decisive war or transforming political integration, Asia's international relations will settle into a pattern of rivalrous interdependence. Asia's states will grow ever more important to each other's growing prosperity and continued development, while, at the same time, their strategic mistrust and power competition will grow. The structure of latent force underpinning rules and institutions in Asia will continue to shift, while tentative measures deliberately short of escalation and war will test how far common understandings of what is permissible can be shifted. It will be an era in which transnational forms of influence, such as investment, infrastructure or diasporas, will become the levers for pursuing rivalries and gaining key advantages in the form of alignments and agreements. It will be a world in which rising powers will try to use regional bodies and trade agreements as mechanisms to build spheres of influence and limit the alignment of smaller states with their rivals. Asia will be the first continent to emerge from under the umbrella of American strategic dominance, which has muted the latent power rivalries of most countries for seven decades. Left to their own devices and suspended uncertainly between war and integration, Asia's jostling powers will develop their own logics and mutual understandings of international relations.

Competition is already well underway in the South China Sea and Bay of Bengal, as well as on the South Asian and West Pacific peninsulas. These are the foundational struggles of Asia's two giants, so fixated on their own geopolitical limitations and the strategic designs of the other. While India has long resented and feared China's support for Pakistan, Beijing itself has begun to take very seriously India's capacity to use its growing naval power to threaten China's energy lifelines through the Indian Ocean. The two latent spheres of competition lie at either end of Asia: in the Indo-Pacific peninsula and the Arabian Sea.

As the Indian and Pacific oceans become more entwined as economic and strategic domains, the benefits that will accrue to a power able to dominate the Indo-Pacific peninsula will be enormous. Allies and bases in the peninsula will allow a power to project its will into both oceans, while threatening its rivals' capacities to freely traverse them.

Further west, the Arabian Sea washes against Asia's great energy source, itself controlled by internally fragile and externally suspicious states. Here, the ebbing of American dominance will be most acutely felt. The United States has long been the weary titan in West Asia, realising that its forces are all that stand between stability and all-out power competition for the region's crucial hydrocarbon reserves. But American dominance has been a self-wasting asset, provoking local reactions that make its commitments increasingly costly in terms of blood, dollars and public support at home. Now, West Asia is beset by a bipolar rivalry between the region's two great powers Shiite Iran and Sunni Saudi Arabia, as well as a fundamentalist insurgency that threatens both. The demands on America's pre-eminence are multiple and unrequited, even as the United States and its allies in Europe are less and less dependent on the region's energy reserves. In the shortfall of American responses, its dissatisfied regional allies increasingly look to their own solutions while its regional enemies grow ever bolder. It is a chessboard that looks more and more open to the growing strategic purchase of Asia's great powers, which are themselves more dependent on West Asian energy and likely worried by the region's rising chaos. And what will alarm Asia's great powers even more than the region's own bipolar rivalry and rising insurgency is the sudden appearance of one of their Asian rivals as a security provider in the region.

Asia and World Order

It seems that Asia will have more than enough to occupy its energies within its own coastlines for the foreseeable future. Surely the rest of the world can simply go about its business while Asia's powers are consumed by their rivalrous interdependence? As long as they keep supplying the rest of the world with high-quality manufacturing and low-cost services, and keep away from waging major war against each other, does it really matter to the rest of the world that Asian states don't trust one another and are increasingly jealous of each other?

The prospect of the rest of the world being unaffected by Asia's patterns of connections and rivalries is small. In our globalised world, where tightening connections mean that even remote events can have very big consequences, a continent with over 60 per cent of the world's population and soon to produce over half of the world's economic activity will have impacts far beyond its own shores. Even if Asia's powers direct their jealousies and anxieties inwards to their own continent, the collateral impact of their competitions and collaborations will spread to other continents. Responsible for two-thirds of the global growth in energy demand until 2035, Asia's developing economies will be the single biggest influence on the trajectory of the world's energy markets in the decades ahead. Not to mention the impact of Asia's carbon emissions on the planetary challenge of climate change. With two-thirds of the world's middle classes and responsibility for 40 per cent of global consumption, by 2030 Asia's economic fortunes will set the terms of the world's economic health. It will be in Asia also that the future of nuclear non-proliferation is decided. If countries such as Iran, Japan, South Korea, Taiwan and Saudi Arabia opt to develop nuclear deterrents, the world could be headed for a new precarious, multi-sided balance of terror.

These will be just some of Asia's gravitational effects on the rest of the world even if the mobilising giants that occupy this continent remain quiescent and continentally focused. On current evidence, it could be argued that this is their stance. While China and India remain obsessed with the challenges bequeathed them by the geography of postwar territorial settlements, their neighbours seem increasingly fixated on the potential of these giants and the long-term prospects of stabilising American power in the region. Indeed, Asia's powers, large and small, seem to have little vision beyond their immediate interests and little capacity or interest in prosecuting larger initiatives. Where they have been impactful in global affairs has been with their power to say no and to block others – on climate change, trade or financial regulation.[10] A very substantial shadow falls between what is expected of Asia's rising powers in global affairs and what they have been willing and able to deliver.

To take this as an enduring characteristic rather than a passing phase would be a heroic assumption. It is hard to think of a major power in world history that has not been tentative and near-sighted in its approach to international affairs during the early stages of its power and wealth. As power grows, so does impatience with aspects of the world they grudgingly accepted when they were poor and weak. Great powers are narcissistic creatures, given to believing their wealth and strength derive from superior ways of organising the world within their borders – and inevitably they begin to think that this is how the world should be ordered beyond their borders also. It is not long before they come to believe that the world should be organised to accommodate the needs and rhythms of their society and economy.

As we have seen, the circumstances of their rise have imbued Asia's powers with four overriding preoccupations concerning the rest of the world. The first is *access*. Asia's great era of economic development occurred decades or even centuries after the societies of North America and Europe developed, prevailed in imperialism and war, and explored, acquired and ordered the rest of the world according to their preferences. So concentrated are the world's assets in the hands of a few societies that many policymakers in Asia are sceptical that these societies will voluntarily allow additional countries to enjoy the benefits of development and wealth – particularly since the populations of Asia's rising powers by far outnumber those of the already developed countries. It is ironic, one hears in some Asian capitals, that concerns about resource depletion, agricultural overexploitation, waste build-up and carbon pollution have arisen after western countries have successfully developed. And so a strategic claustrophobia has developed among Asia's rising powers: a feeling that with each success they confront new limits and jealousies, and a fear that those who have stitched up the global economy could one day simply decide to cut the rising powers off from what they need to succeed.

Second, Asian countries are increasingly preoccupied with being accorded *respect* for their status, achievements and opinions. Most have a sense of historical greatness that translates into a contemporary sense of importance. While this is most pronounced in China, India and Indonesia, their smaller neighbours have too strong a sense of cultural pride and historical greatness simply to accept a subordinate role in a hierarchical order in Asia. The demand for respect extends to relations with the west also, particularly in countries such as Malaysia and Myanmar where memories of colonial domination are strongest. Asian sensibilities particularly bristle at criticisms from the west or pressures to change the way Asians do things; in this sense the demand for respect translates into an injunction to be left alone to order their domestic affairs as they see fit.

Third, Asian states are increasingly demanding a *voice* in determining how institutions and rules work in the world. For much of the period in which their growth trajectories were taking off, Asia's states were content with a relatively quiescent role in global forums. Even Japan, for four decades the world's second-largest economy, accepted a less influential role in governing world financial affairs than America or Europe. As their gross domestic products have risen, the puny voting weights accorded to Asian powers in global institutions such as the IMF have started to look downright embarrassing, yet despite calls for reform and rebalancing of these institutions, including by the G20, it has proven difficult for the United States and European countries to cede any formal or informal power.[11] Facing so little apparent fairness or goodwill within global councils, Asia's largest states are often forced into simple obstruction to initiatives that they believe will threaten their development trajectories. The other strategy they have begun to adopt is to create alternative institutions to help compensate for what they fear will be unsympathetic responses from global institutions if things go wrong in Asia.

The fourth preoccupation of Asian states is *assurance*. Despite their rise, there is no shortage of paranoia in Asia's capital cities – a nagging anxiety that all of their success could, through accident or design, be suddenly stripped away. On one view, Japan's experience with sudden and rapid growth is a cautionary tale. In the 1980s, as Japan's industrial growth outpaced that of the United States and European countries, it began to be seen as a threat. The United States – Japan's treaty ally – banned the export of sensitive satellite technologies to Japan, while beefy American congressmen smashed piles of Japanese-made televisions with baseball bats. Washington used its leverage to force Tokyo to sign the 1985 Plaza Accord to weight the trading advantages in its favour.[12] It was only when the Japanese economy began to flatline in the 1990s that Tokyo was welcomed back into the fold. Whether this is a fair reading of history or not, stories such as this play into fears that Asia's developing powers will somehow be reined in before they can pose too great a threat to the west. Encirclement and containment anxieties are rarely far from the surface in Beijing and New Delhi, and a great deal of effort is spent trying to hedge against such occurrences. Finding a sense of existential security will be a preoccupation not just for China and India but for most of their neighbours too.

Access, respect, voice and assurance will be the underlying drivers of Asia's rising powers as they wield influence in the twenty-first century. The question often asked about China – whether it will become a power that defends the global status quo or seeks to overthrow that status quo – could also be asked of its fast-developing neighbours. Asian powers' four preoccupations suggest the answer to this question is neither. Worries about access and respect suggest that there is much in the status quo that Asian states would like to see changed, but that the demands for voice and reassurance are strong enough to banish all thoughts of a revolutionary redesign of current rules and institutions. Rather than starting at the global level, there are strong indications that Asian powers are focusing their initial energies on ensuring that key relationships in the world close to their borders are consistent with their need for access, respect, voice and assurance. Whether it be President Xi Jinping's statement that China will secure its growth by creating a 'more enabling international environment', or New Delhi's long-held policy of excluding from its environs interests that could be inimical to India's interests, or ASEAN's proclamation of a 'zone of peace, freedom and neutrality' in Southeast Asia, there is a strong urge to reorder important dynamics within regions or subregions. We have also seen the need for access and reassurance prompt Asia's state-owned energy and minerals companies to invest in other continents, while their foreign ministry colleagues build close relations with the governments in question.[13] Those elements of the global order that seem particularly threatening are being quietly dismantled within some states: witness, for example, China's slow strangling of western internet companies in Chinese cyberspace while allowing Chinese companies more aligned with Beijing's political preferences to thrive.[14]

As their relative power and wealth grows, so Asian powers' efforts to build spheres of influence and assurance will intensify. This will have major implications for the world we and our children will live in. Since the voyages of Columbus and da Gama in the late fifteenth century, humans have existed within a single global international order. The first phase of globalism can be called *incorporation*, because it involved the extension of Europe's rivalries and industrial–commercial dynamics to all other inhabited continents. The imperial age, in effect, incorporated the rest of the world into Europe's logics and dynamics, while stamping out the various regional power orders that had existed until that era. In the twentieth century came the age of *emulation*, whereby the colonisers were sent packing but their methods of organising societies, politics and economies were adopted by the newly independent states, as were their methods of dealing with other states. To deal with the sudden loss of direct political control over other societies, Europe and the United States instituted a system of *stabilisation*, a third form of globalism. Stabilisation manifested in an intensive period of forming collaborative institutions such as the United Nations and encoding certain liberal norms to stave off another destructive bout of global war and economic instability. The Bretton Woods institutions were formed to preserve the global reach of the postwar economy, despite the independence of former colonies, and to place a buffer of stabilising rules and institutions around the unpredictability of economic cycles.[15] While many of the new states were not parties to these institutions, their architects were strong believers in the socialising powers of the institutions they were building.

With the rise of great powers in Asia – Japan, China, India, Russia and perhaps, in time, Indonesia – we need to question the longevity not only of the content of international order but also of its global extent. Their demand for access and respect, their frustration at the persisting lack of meaningful voice and their need for reassurance mean that, increasingly, Asia's powers are looking past global institutions to construct alternatives that are more conducive to their interests and opinions. Already the Chinese president has started to talk of 'Asian solutions to Asian problems' and extol the virtues of a new 'harmonious' international order – harmonised to China's preferences, of course.[16] With the dysfunction of global institutions and the vanishing prospect they can be reformed to better reflect international power realities, this century's international relations could see a gradual crumbling of the globalism that has prevailed for half a millennium. The next phase of world order could very well be one of *disarticulation*, whereby Europe, America and Asia's great powers compete to build zones of influence and deference around their borders and with regions and countries of importance, such as resource suppliers. In between would be stretched an increasingly threadbare tissue of global rules and institutions.

Thinkers such as Walter Lippmann and Winston Churchill proposed during the last phases of the Second World War that spheres of influence policed by great powers would be a surer way to a stable world than globalism. Writing in defence of the American invasion of the Dominican Republic in 1965, Lippmann argued:

> Recognition of spheres of influence is a true alternative to globalism. It is the alternative to communist globalism which proclaims a universal revolution. It is the alternative to anticommunist globalism that promises to fight anti-communist wars everywhere. The acceptance of spheres of influence has been the dominant foundation of the détente in Europe between the Soviet Union and the West. Eventually it will provide the formula of co-existence between Red China and the United States.[17]

But the world has avoided reverting to spheres of influence as the basis for international order for very good reasons. A disarticulated world would be one of separate trade and investment blocs, regional security alignments and different communications and information ecologies. It would be a world in which the easy globalism we enjoy would fade away into incompatibilities and incomprehension. It would most likely be a world less prosperous than we are used to and which would find global problems much harder to address.

The choice between globalism and disarticulation lies as much with smaller states as it does with the great powers. Spheres of influence require at least a measure of compliance from smaller countries if they are to be meaningful. And in the smaller Asian states' need for access, respect, voice and assurance lies a scepticism, if not outright defiance, of their giant neighbours' attempts to construct zones of compatibility around them. It is in a world of robust globalism – preferably modified to better reflect non-western preferences – that smaller states will best preserve their advantages and options for dealing on more equal terms with great powers. A new, more robust, more representative globalism would be a truly valuable contribution to world order from an increasingly restless continent.

ACKNOWLEDGEMENTS

Writing a book – at least for me – is essentially a work of alchemy: extracting, arranging and transmuting an array of disparate thoughts, images, arguments and jottings into a (hopefully) coherent narrative. My intellectual debts are consequently to all the people, settings and places that provoked, inspired and indulged the questions, arguments and connections that are at the core of this book.

I am grateful to the Australian Centre for Defence and Strategic Studies, which, on short notice, asked me to give a lecture to a hall full of military officers from across the world, titled 'The Indo-Pacific as a Strategic System'. In that hurriedly prepared presentation, and the rich discussion afterwards, were the foundational questions that inspired this book. How does wealth and power affect Asian states' sense of security and entitlement? Is enmeshment with the regional and global economy necessarily a pacifying influence? How does Asia's geography shape rivalry and conflict?

Further questions, connections and intellectual perambulations were tested on audiences and interlocutors around the world: at the Nordic Institute of Asian Studies in Copenhagen; the East–West Center in Washington; the Institute for Defence Studies and Analyses and the Observer Research Foundation in New Delhi;

the Norwegian Institute of International Affairs in Oslo; Konrad-Adenauer-Stiftung in Berlin; Waseda University in Tokyo; UI in Stockholm; the foreign and defence ministries in Australia, Norway, Sweden and Finland; the Office of National Assessments in Canberra; to sea power and maritime defence conferences in Sydney and Taipei. Perhaps the greatest influence was my colleagues at the Australian National University, who provide a constant rich ecology of knowledge, provocations and insights on politics and strategy in Asia and the Pacific.

I have been lucky to be helped by people who directed me to the information I needed. The Sea Power Centre in Canberra, facilitated by Justin Jones and Andrew Forbes, provided a treasure trove of information and analysis on maritime strategy. Ramesh Paudel guided me gently through the complex world of statistics and research on Asian economic integration and interdependence. Rod Murchison did the same in the equally arcane – for me at least – world of military acquisitions in Asia. Olivia Cable was as cheerful as she was resourceful in chasing down constant requests for obscure statistics or facts. My colleagues Ryan Manuel, Amy King, David Envall, Nich Farrelly and Brendan Taylor were generous in pointing me in the right direction or suggesting readings to explore a new avenue of inquiry.

Danielle Cave was extremely generous with her time in reading and providing extensive comments on large segments of the manuscript.

My thanks to Margaret Gee for her counsel and encouragement over many cups of tea. Also to Chris Feik at Black Inc. for his understanding and forbearance as I missed deadline after deadline. And to Gill Smith for her careful and sympathetic editing.

The greatest support and inspiration came from the 'Home Office'. Sheridan, Oskar and Felix kept me sane and grounded, and endured for too long my disappearances into the study, my distracted and divided attention, my travels, my ill-temper and the constant presence of my laptop on family holidays. I wrote this book for Oskar and Felix, who, for better or worse, will grow up to live in, and help to shape, the world this book describes.

ENDNOTES

Preface

1   Hillary Clinton, "America's Pacific Century", *Foreign Policy*, 11 October 2011

2   US Department of Defense, "Sustaining US Global Leadership: Priorities for 21st Century Defense," p. 2

3   James R. Fichter, *So Great a Proffit: How the East Indies Trade Transformed Anglo-American Capitalism*. Cambridge: Harvard University Press, 2010

Introduction

1   James R Holmes, 'Japan and China: Tensions mounting', *The Diplomat*, 6 February 2013.

2   Robert Ayson & Desmond Ball, 'Can a Sino-Japanese War Be Controlled?', *Survival*, Vol. 56, No. 6, December 2014 – January 2015, pp. 135–66.

3   Quoted in SCM Paine, *The Sino-Japanese War of 1894–1895: Perceptions, Power and Primacy*, Cambridge: Cambridge University Press, 2003, pp. 192–3.

4   Calculations based on Angus Maddison's historical data; see The Maddison Project, www.ggdc.net/maddison/maddison-project/home.htm, 2013 version.

5   WJ Macpherson, *The Economic Development of Japan, c. 1868–1941*, Basingstoke: Macmillan, 1987.

6   Paine, 2003, pp. 81–2.

7   Quoted in Paine, 2003, p. 314.

Chapter 1 Peace Dividends

1   My account of the fall of Saigon draws heavily on Olivier Todd, *Cruel April: The Fall of Saigon*, New York: WW Norton, 1987.

2   Daniel Bell, 'The end of American exceptionalism', *The Public Interest*, Fall, 1975, reprinted in Daniel Bell, *The Winding Passage: Essays and Sociological Journeys 1960–1980*, Cambridge, Mass.: Abt Books, 1980.

3   Frederik Logevall & Andrew Preston (eds) *Nixon in the World: American Foreign Relations, 1969–1977*, New York: Oxford University Press, 2008.

4   Robert S Litwak, *Détente and the Nixon Doctrine: American Foreign Policy and the Pursuit of Stability, 1969–1976*, Cambridge: Cambridge University Press, 1984.

5   Richard Nixon, 'Informal remarks in Guam with newsmen', 25 July 1969, online by Gerhard Peters and John T Woolley, The American Presidency Project, www.presidency.ucsb.edu/ws/?pid=2140.

6   Richard Nixon, 'US foreign policy for the 1970s: A new strategy for peace', 18 February 1970, Vol. I, Foundations of Foreign Policy, 1969–1972, Document 60, *Foreign Relations of the United States, 1969–1976*, https://history.state.gov/historicaldocuments/frus1969-76v01/d60.

7   Ronald C Keith, *The Diplomacy of Zhou Enlai*, London: Macmillan, 1989.

8   Lorenz M Luthi, *The Sino-Soviet Split: Cold War in the Communist World*, Princeton: Princeton University Press, 2008.

9   Qiang Zhai, *China and the Vietnam Wars, 1950–1975*, Chapel Hill: University of North Carolina Press, 2000.

10 James Mann, *About Face: A History of America's Curious Relationship with China, From Nixon to Clinton*, New York: Alfred A Knopf, 1999.

11 Nancy Bernkopf Tucker (ed.) *China Confidential: American Diplomats and Sino-American Relations, 1945–1996*, New York: Columbia University Press, 2001.

12 King C Chen, *China's War with Vietnam, 1979: Issues, Decisions, Implications*, Stanford: Hoover Institution Press, 1987.

13 Robert G Sutter, *Chinese Foreign Policy: Developments After Mao*, New York: Praeger, 1985.

14 Richard Sisson & Leo E Rose, *War and Secession: Pakistan, India and the Creation of Bangladesh*, Berkeley: University of California Press, 1990.

15 Raymond L Brown, *Anwar al-Sadat and the October War*, Santa Monica: California Seminar on Arms Control and Foreign Policy, 1980.

16 Saad Shazly, *The Crossing of Suez: The October War 1973*, London: Third World Centre for Research and Publication, 1980.

17 Misagh Parsa, *The Social Origins of the Iranian Revolution*, Brunswick: Rutgers University Press, 1989.

18 Joseph J Collins, *The Soviet Invasion of Afghanistan: A Study in the Use of Force in Soviet Foreign Policy*, Lexington Books, 1986.

19 Robert F Miller, *Soviet Foreign Policy Today: Gorbachev and the New Foreign Policy Thinking*, New York: Unwin Hyman, 1991.

20 Alice Lyman Miller & Richard Wich, *Becoming Asia: Change and Continuity in Asian International Relations Since World War II*, Stanford: Stanford University Press, 2011.

21 Gunnar Myrdal, *Asian Drama: An Inquiry Into the Poverty of Nations*, New York: Twentieth Century Fund, 1968.

22 Lawrence MacDonald (ed.), *The East Asian Miracle: Economic Growth and Public Policy*, World Bank Policy Research Report, New York: Oxford University Press, 1993.

23 GDP growth data is taken from the International Monetary Fund's World Economic Outlook Database, April 2015, at www.imf.org/external/pubs/ft/weo/2015/01/weodata/index.aspx.

24 Anis Chowdhury & Iyanatul Islam (eds), *Handbook on the Northeast and Southeast Asian Economies*, Cheltenham: Edward Elgar, 2007.

25 Thanat Khoman, 'ASEAN: Conception and evolution', in KS Sandhu et al. (eds) *The ASEAN Reader, Singapore: Institute for Southeast Asian Studies, 1992*; Michael Leifer, ASEAN and the Security of Southeast Asia, London: Routledge, 1989.

26 MC Abad Jr, 'The Association of Southeast Asian Nations: Challenges and responses' in Michael Wesley (ed.), *The Regional Organizations of the Asia–Pacific: Exploring Institutional Change*, Basingstoke: Palgrave Macmillan, 2003.

27 Goh Chok Tong, 'ASEAN–US Relations', speech to the ASEAN – United States Partnership Conference, New York, 7 September 2000.

28 Robert Gilpin, *The Multinational Corporation and the National Interest*, Washington, DC: US Government Printing Office, 1973.

29 Indermit Singh Gill & Homi J Kharas, An *East Asian Renaissance: Ideas for Economic Growth*, Washington: World Bank, 2007.

30 Karen Ward, *The World in 2050*, HSBC Global Research, January 2012.

31 Willem Buiter & Ebrahim Rhabari, 'Global growth generators: Moving beyond "emerging markets" and "BRIC" ', *Citibank Global Economics View*, January 2011.

32 Dominic Wilson, *Dreaming with BRICs: The Path to 2050*, Goldman Sachs Global Investment Research, October 2003.

33 Australian Government, *Australia in the Asian Century*, White Paper, Commonwealth of Australia, October 2012.

34 Kishore Mahbubani, *The New Asian Hemisphere: The Irresistible Shift of Global Power to the East*, New York: Public Affairs, 2008, p. 2.

Chapter 2 Significant Others

1 Melvyn C Goldstein, *A History of Modern Tibet*, Berkeley: University of California Press, 2014.

2 Edward Dalton, *Tribal Worlds of the Eastern Himalaya and Indo-Burma Borderlands*, Bangkok: White Lotus, 2007.

3 Jason Neelis, *Early Buddhist Transmission and Trade Networks*, Leiden: Brill, 2011; Ralph Kautz (ed.), *Aspects of the Maritime Silk Road: From the Persian Gulf to the East China Sea*, Wiesbaden: Harrassowitz Verlag, 2010; Johan Elverskog, *Buddhism and Islam on the Silk Road*, Philadelphia: University of Pennsylvania Press, 2010.

4 Jack Weatherford, *Genghis Khan and the Making of the Modern World*, New York: Crown, 2004.

5 Janet L Abu-Lughod, *Before European Hegemony: The World System AD 1250–1350*, New York: Oxford University Press, 1989.

6 Alan Hodgart, *The Economics of European Imperialism*, London: Edward Arnold, 1977.

7 John R Fisher, *The Economic Aspects of Spanish Imperialism in America, 1492–1810*, Liverpool: Liverpool University Press, 1997; JP Cain, *British Imperialism: Innovation and Expansion, 1688–1914*, New York: Longman, 1993.

8 Bailey Diffie, *Foundations of the Portuguese Empire, 1415–1580*, Minneapolis: University of Minnesota Press, 1977.

9 Sanjay Subrahmanyam, *The Portuguese Empire in Asia, 1500–1700: A Political and Economic History*, London: Longman, 1993.

10 Francisco Bethencourt & Diogo Ramada Curto (eds), *Portuguese Oceanic Expansion, 1400–1800*, Cambridge: Cambridge University Press, 2007.

11 CR Boxer, *The Dutch Seaborne Empire, 1600–1800*, London: Hutchinson, 1965.

12 MN Pearson, *The World of the Indian Ocean, 1500–1800*, Burlington: Ashgate, 2005.

13 Robert Johnson, *British Imperialism*, Houndmills: Macmillan, 2007.

14 Raymond F Betts, *Europe Overseas: The Phases of Imperialism*, New York: Basic Books, 1968.

15 Donald G McCloud, *System and Process in Southeast Asia: The Evolution of a Region*, Boulder: Westview Press, 1986.

16 Dean Acheson, quoted in Cynthia Ann Watson (ed.), *US National Security: A Reference Handbook*, Santa Barbara: ABC-CLIO, 2002, pp. 159–60.

17 Tony Cavoli, Siona Listokin & Ramkishen S Rajan (eds), *Issues in Governance, Growth and Globalization in Asia*, Hackensack: World Scientific, 2014.

18 Razeen Sally, *Economic Integration in Asia: The Track Record and Prospects*, ECIPE Occasional Paper No. 2, Brussels: European Centre for International Political Economy, 2010.

19 Yuko Kikuchi, *Japanese Modernisation and Mingei Theory: Cultural Nationalism and Oriental Orientalism*, New York: RoutledgeCurzon, 2004.

20 Harald Fuess (ed.), *The Japanese Empire in East Asia and its Postwar Legacy*, Munich: Iudicium, 1998.

21 Jun Uchida, *Brokers of Empire: Japanese Settler Colonialism in Korea, 1876–1945*, Cambridge: Harvard University Press, 2011.

22 James C Scott, *Seeing Like a State: How Certain Schemes to Improve the Human Condition Have Failed*, New Haven: Yale University Press, 1998.

23 Sven Saaler & J Victor Koschmann (eds), *Pan-Asianism in Modern Japanese History: Colonialism, Regionalism and Borders*, London: Routledge, 2007.

24 Frank B Tipton, *The Rise of Asia: Economics, Society and Politics in Contemporary Asia*, Melbourne: Macmillan, 1998.

25 Michael Wesley, 'The Asian Development Bank', in Michael Wesley (ed.), *The Regional Organizations of the Asia-Pacific: Exploring Institutional Change*, Basingstoke: Palgrave Macmillan, 2003.

26 Prema-chandra Athukorala, *Production Networks and Trade Patterns in East Asia: Regionalization or Globalization?*, ADB Working Paper Series on Regional Economic Integration, No. 56, Asian Development Bank, August 2010.

27 Prema-chandra Athukorala, 'Asian trade and investment: Trends and patterns', in Prema-chandra Athukorala (ed.), *The Rise of Asia : Trade and Investment in Global Perspective*, New York: Routledge, 2010.

28 Linghe Ye & Masato Abe, *The Impacts of Natural Disasters on Global Supply Chains*, ARTNeT Working Paper No. 115, Bangkok: UN ESCAP, 2012.

29 All energy figures are taken from the International Energy Agency, *World Energy Outlook 2014*, Paris: OECD/IEA, 2014.

30 All energy figures are taken from the International Energy Agency, *World Energy Outlook 2014*, Paris: OECD/IEA, 2014.

31 Amy Myers Jaffe, Kenneth B Medlock & Ronald Soligo, *The status of World Oil Reserves: Conventional and Unconventional Resources in the Future Supply Mix*, James A Baker III Institute for Public Policy of Rice University, March 2011.

32 Philip Andrews-Speed, Sumit Ganguly, Manjeet S Pardesi, et al., *The New Energy Silk Road: The Growing Asia – Middle East Energy Nexus*, The National Bureau of Asian Research, October 2009.

33 Saad Alshahrani & Ali Alsadiq, *Economic Growth and Government Spending in Saudi Arabia*, IMF Working Paper No. 14/3, International Monetary Fund, 2014.

34 Naser Al-Tamimi, *China – Saudi Arabia Relations: Economic Partnership or Strategic Alliance?*, Discussion Paper, Durham: HH Sheikh Nasser Al-Sabah Programme, Durham University, 2012.

35 PricewaterhouseCoopers, *Developing Infrastructure in Asia Pacific: Outlook, Challenges and Solutions*, PricewaterhouseCoopers Services LLP, 2014.

36 Asian Development Bank, *Infrastructure for a Seamless Asia*, Manila: ADB, 2009.

37 Neil Thomas, 'Rhetoric and reality – Xi Jinping's Australia policy', *The China Story Journal*, Australian Centre on China and the World, 15 March 2015, www.thechinastory.org/2015/03/rhetoric-and-reality-xi-jinpings-australia-policy/.

38 Alexander Cooley, 'The new great game in Central Asia', *Foreign Affairs*, Council on Foreign Relations, 7 August 2012.

39 Homi Kharas, *The Emerging Middle Class in Developing Countries*, OECD Development Centre Working Paper No. 285, OECD, January 2010.

40 Thorstein Veblen, *The Theory of the Leisure Class*, New York: Oxford University Press, 2007.

41 UN World Tourism Organization, *Tourism Highlights 2014*, UNWTO, 2014.

Chapter 3 Compulsive Ambition

1 Dennis O Flynn, *World Silver and Monetary Histories in the 16th and 17th Centuries*, Aldershot: Varorium, 1996.

2 Charles O Hucker, *The Ming Dynasty: Its Origins and Evolving Institutions*, Ann Arbor: University of Michigan Press, 1978.

3 Mi Chu Wiens, *Socioeconomic Change During the Ming Dynasty in the Kiangnan Area*, PhD dissertation, Harvard University, 1973.

4 The story of the Suzhou riot is drawn from Pei-kai Cheng, Michael Lestz, Jonathan D Spence (eds), *The Search for Modern China: A Documentary Collection*, New York: Norton, 1999.

5 Quoted in Cheng, Lestz, Spence (eds), 1999.

6 John W Dardess, *Ming China 1368–1644*, Lanham: Rowman & Littlefield, 2012.

7 Jiang Yonglin, *The Mandate of Heaven and the Great Ming Code*, Seattle: University of Washington Press, 2011.

8 Quoted in Li Kangying, *The Ming Maritime Trade Policy in Transition, 1368 to 1567*, Wiesbaden: Harrassowitz Verlag, 2010, p. 7.

9 Bruce Swanson, *Eighth Voyage of the Dragon: A History of China's Quest for Seapower*, Annapolis: Naval Institute Press, 1982.

10 Itoh Mayumi, *Globalization of Japan: Japanese Sakoku Mentality and US Efforts to Open Japan*, New York: St Martin's Press, 1998.

11 Donald N Clark, *Korea in World History*, Ann Arbor: University of Michigan Press, 2012.

12 Bjoern Dressel & Michael Wesley, 'Asian states in crisis', *Strategic Analysis*, Vol. 38, No. 4, July 2014.

13 Peter Drysdale (ed.), *The New Economy in East Asia and the Pacific*, New York: Routledge, 2004.

14 United Nations ESCAP, 'Urbanization trends in Asia and the Pacific', UN ESCAP Factsheet, November 2013, www.unescapsdd.org/files/documents/SPPS-Factsheet-urbanization-v5.pdf.

15 Dean Forbes, *Urbanisation in Asia*, Canberra: AusAID, 1998.

16 Ghulam Akhmat & Yo Bochun, 'Rapidly changing dynamics of urbanization in China: Escalating regional inequalities and urban management problems', *Journal of Sustainable Development*, Vol. 3 No. 2, June 2010.

17 Shirish Sankhe, et al., *India's Urban Awakening: Building Inclusive Cities, Sustaining Economic Growth*, McKinsey Global Institute, April 2010.

18 Michael Spence, Patricia Clarke Annez & Robert M Buckley (eds), *Urbanization and Growth*, Washington: World Bank, 2009.

19 Wang Fei-ling, *Organizing Through Division and Exclusion: China's Hukou System*, Stanford: Stanford University Press, 2005.

20 Tom Miller, *China's Urban Billion*, New York: Zed Books, 2012.

21 KC Roy, *Economic Development in China, India and East Asia: Managing Change in the Twenty-First Century*, Cheltenham: Edward Elgar, 2012.

22 Adam Drewnowski & Barry M Popkin, 'The nutrition transition: New trends in the global diet', *Nutrition Reviews*, Vol. 55, No. 2, 1997.

23 Zhu Xiaodong, 'Understanding China's growth: Past, present, and future', *Journal of Economic Perspectives*, Vol. 26, No. 4, Fall 2012.

24 Lucy Hornby, 'China scythes food self-sufficiency policy', *Financial Times*, 11 February 2014.

25 All energy figures are taken from the International Energy Agency, *World Energy Outlook 2014*, Paris: OECD/IEA, 2014.

26 Shahid Khandker (ed.), *Impact of the Asian Financial Crisis Revisited*, Washington: World Bank Institute, 2002.

27 Justin Yifu Lin, *The China Miracle: Development Strategy and Economic Reform*, Hong Kong: Chinese University Press, 1996.

28 Anna Jankowska, Ame Norgengast & Jose Ramon Perea, *The Middle Income Trap: Comparing Asian and Latin American Experiences*, OECD Development Centre Policy Insight, May 2012; Jesus Felipe, Utsav Kumar & Reynold Galope, 'Middle Income Transitions: Trap or Myth?' ADB Economics Working Papers Series No. 421, Asian Development Bank, November 2014.

29 Hal Hill & Thee Kian Wie, 'Indonesian universities: Rapid growth, major challenges', in Daniel Suryadarma & Gavin W Jones (eds), *Education in Indonesia*, Singapore: ISEAS, 2012.

30 Pawan Agarwal, *Indian Higher Education: Envisioning the Future*, New Dehli: Sage, 2009.

31 Shi Li & Chunbing Xing, *China's Higher Education Expansion and its Labor Market Consequences*, IZA Discussion Papers No. 4974, Institute for the Study of Labor, May 2010.

32 Yu He & Yinhua Mai, 'Higher Education Expansion in China and the "Ant Tribe" Problem', *Higher Education Policy*, 17 June 2014.

33 Zhou Xiaochuan, Statement on the International Financial System, Council on Foreign Relations, 23 March 2009, www.cfr.org/china/zhou-xiaochuans-statement-reforming-international-monetary-system/p18916.

34 John Kehoe, 'Rajan Clashes With Bernanke Over QE Taper', *Australian Financial Review*, 11 April 2014.

35 Outbound Investment Development Report 2010, MOFCOM, 1 November 2010, as reported in *Beijing Review*, 25 November 2010.

36 Robert Zoellick, Whither China: From Membership to Responsibility?, Remarks to National Committee on US–China Relations, New York, 21 September 2005.

37 Stijn Classens & M Ayhan Kose, *Financial Crises: Explanations, Types, and Implications*, IMF Working Paper 13/28, International Monetary Fund, January 2013.

38 Quoted in Thomas, 2015.

Chapter 4 Restless Souls

1 Robert Grant Irving, *Imperial Summer: Lutyens, Baker and Imperial Delhi*, New Haven: Yale University Press, 1981.

2 Shankar Sharan, *Fifty Years After the Asian Relations Conference*, New Delhi: Tibetan Parliamentary and Policy Research Centre, 1997.

3 JA McCallum, 'The Asian Relations Conference', *The Australian Quarterly*, June 1947.

4 Jawaharlal Nehru, Inaugural speech to the Asian Relations Conference, New Delhi, 23 March 1947, reprinted in Sharan, 1997.

5 Jawaharlal Nehru, reprinted in Sharan, 1997.

6 Amitav Acharya, 'The idea of Asia', *Asia Policy*, Vol. 9, No. 1, January 2010.

7 Clifford Geertz, *Negara: The Theatre State in Nineteenth Century Bali*, Princeton: Princeton University Press, 1980, p. 18.

8 Jacques Gernet, *A History of Chinese Civilization*, Cambridge: Cambridge University Press, 1972.

9 Donald G McCloud, *System and Process in Southeast Asia: The Evolution of a Region*, Boulder: Westview Press, 1986.

10 Thongchai Winichakul, 'Trying to locate Southeast Asia from its navel: Where is Southeast Asian studies in Thailand?', in Paul H Kratoska, Remco Raben & Henk Schulte Nordholt (eds), *Locating Southeast Asia: Geographies of Knowledge and Politics of Space*, Athens: Ohio University Press, 2005.

11 Geertz, 1980.

12 Alexander Vuving, 'Operated by world views and interfaced by world

orders: Traditional and modern Sino-Vietnamese relations', in Anthony Reid & Zheng Yangwen (eds), *Negotiating Asymmetry: China's Place in Asia*, Singapore: NUS Press, 2009, p. 82.

13 Leif-Erik Easley, 'Korean and Vietnamese national identities: Navigating Chinese and American power', in Joon-Woo Park, Gi-Wook Shin & Donald W Kayser (eds), *The Identity and Regional Policy of South Korea and Vietnam*, Washington, DC: The Brookings Institution, 2013.

14 Benedict Anderson, *Imagined Communities: Reflections on the Origins and Spread of Nationalism*, London: Verso, 1991, p. 150.

15 Rotem Kowner & Walter Demel (eds), *Race and Racism in Modern East Asia: Western and Eastern Constructions*, Leiden: Brill, 2013.

16 Anthony Reid, 'Introduction: Negotiating asymmetry – brothers, friends and enemies' in Reid & Zheng, 2009, p. 18.

17 Seo-Hyun Park, 'Small states and the search for sovereignty in Sinocentric Asia: Japan and Korea in the late nineteenth century', in Reid & Zheng, 2009, p. 32.

18 Gerrit W Gong, *The Standard of 'Civilization' in International Society*, Oxford: Clarendon Press, 1984.

19 Anthony Reid, *Imperial Alchemy: Nationalism and Political Identity in Southeast Asia*, Cambridge: Cambridge University Press, 2010.

20 For a fuller discussion of these processes see Michael Wesley, 'Asia enters an era of strife', *Far Eastern Economic Review*, Vol. 172, No. 3, April 2009, pp. 14–18.

21 Robert E Elson, *The Idea of Indonesia*, Cambridge: Cambridge University Press, 2008.

22 Wang Gungwu, 'Family and friends: China in a changing Asia', in Reid & Zheng, 2009, p. 225.

23 Takashi Shiraishi (ed.), *Across the Causeway: A Multi-Dimensional Study of Malaysia–Singapore Relations*, Singapore: ISEAS, 2009.

24 Joseph Chin-Yong Liow, *The Politics of Indonesia–Malaysia Relations: One Kin, Two Nations*, London: RoutledgeCurzon, 2005.

25 Quoted in Rizal Sukma, *Indonesia and China: The Politics of a Troubled Relationship*, London: Routledge, 1999, p. 158.

26 Quoted in John Pomfret, 'US Takes a Tougher Line with China', *The Washington Post*, 30 July 2010.

27 Alexander Vuving, 'How experience and identity shape Vietnam's relations with China and the United States', in Park, Shin & Keyser, 2013, p. 60.

28 Terence Roehrig, 'History as a strategic weapon: The Korean and Chinese struggle over Koguryo', *Journal of Asian and African Studies*, Vol. 45, No. 1, February 2010.

29 Peter Hays Gries, 'The Koguryo controversy, national identity, and Sino-Korean relations today', *East Asia*, Vol. 22, No. 4, December 2005.

30 Chen Dingding, 'Domestic politics, national identity, and international conflict: The case of the Koguryo controversy', *Journal of Contemporary China*, Vol. 21, No. 74, March 2012.

31 Kwai-Chung Lo, 'Manipulating historical tensions in east Asian popular culture', in Nissim Otmazgin & Eyal Ben-Ari (eds), *Popular Culture and the State in East and Southeast Asia*, London: Routledge, 2012, p. 185.

32 Kawashima Shin, 'China's re-interpretation of the Chinese world order, 1900–40s', in Reid & Zheng, 2009, p. 147.

33 Vuving, 'Operated by world views and interfaced by world orders', in Reid & Zheng, 2009, p. 82.

34 WJF Jenner, *The Tyranny of History: The Roots of China's Crisis*, Harmondsworth: Allen Lane, 1992, pp. 4–5.

35 Winichakul, in Kratoska, Raben & Nordholt, 2005.

36 Sukma, 1999, p. 95.

37 John W Garver, 'Indo-Chinese rivalry in Indochina', *Asian Survey*, Vol. 27, No. 11, November 1987.

38 Geertz, 1980, p. 62.

39 CP Fitzgerald, *The Southern Expansion of the Chinese People*, New York: Praeger, 1972.

40 John F Richards, *The Mughal Empire*, New York: Cambridge University Press, 1993.

41 Anthony Reid, *Southeast Asia in the Age of Commerce 1450–1680*, Vols I and II, New Haven: Yale University Press, 1993.

42 Sunil S Amrith, *Crossing the Bay of Bengal: The Furies of Nature and the Fortunes of Migrants*, Cambridge: Harvard University Press, 2013.

43 Michael R Stenson, *Class, Race and Colonialism in West Malaysia*, Vancouver: University of British Columbia Press, 1980.

44 Grant Evans (ed.), *Asia's Cultural Mosaic: An Anthropological Introduction*, New York: Prentice-Hall, 1993.

45 Stein Tonneson & Hans Antlov (eds), *Asian Forms of the Nation*, Richmond: Curzon, 1996.

46 Rajat Ganguly (ed.), *Autonomy and Ethnic Conflict in South and Southeast Asia*, Abingdon: Routledge, 2012.

47 Leo Suryadinata, *Understanding the Ethnic Chinese in Southeast Asia*, Singapore: ISEAS, 2007.

48 Robert Lowry, *The Armed Forces of Indonesia*, Sydney: Allen & Unwin, 1996.

49 Reid, *Imperial Alchemy*, 2010, p. 63.

50 Sukma, 1999, p. 24.

51 Liow, 2005.

52 Kate Hodal & Jonathan Kaiman, 'At least 21 dead in Vietnam anti-China riots over oil rig', *The Guardian*, 16 May 2014.

53 Natasha Hamilton-Hart, 'Indonesia and Singapore: Structure, politics and interests', *Contemporary Southeast Asia*, Vol. 31, No. 2, 2009, pp. 247–71.

54 Liow, 2005.

55 JAC Mackie, *Konfrontasi: The Indonesia–Malaysia Dispute 1963-1966*, Melbourne: Oxford University Press, 1974.

56 Vuving, in Park, Shin & Keyser, 2013, p. 61.

57 David Brewster, *India as an Asia–Pacific Power*, London: Routledge, 2012.

Chapter 5 Fateful Terrains

1 Marcus Scott-Ross, *A Short History of Malacca*, Singapore: Chopmen Enterprises, 1971.

2 John Villiers, *Portuguese Malacca*, Bangkok: Exbaixada de Portugal na Tailandia, 1988.

3 Samuel Wee Tien Wang, British Strategic Interests in the Strait of Malacca 1786–1819, MA thesis, Simon Fraser University, 1992.

4 Colin S Gray, 'Inescapable geography', *Journal of Strategic Studies*, Vol. 22, No. 2–3, 1999.

5 Anthony Reid, *Southeast Asia in the Age of Commerce, 1450–1680*, New Haven: Yale University Press, 1993.

6 Hendrik Spruyt, *The Sovereign State and Its Competitors*, Princeton: Princeton University Press, 1994.

7 Ewan W Anderson, 'Geopolitics: International boundaries as fighting places', in Colin S Gray & Geoffrey Sloan (eds), *Geopolitics, Geography and Strategy*, Abingdon: Routledge, 2013, pp. 130–1.

8 Halford Mackinder, *The Scope and Methods of Geography and the Geographical Pivot of History*, London: Royal Geographical Society, 1951.

9 Ralf Emmers, *Geopolitics and Maritime Territorial Disputes in East Asia*, Abingdon: Routledge, 2010.

10 Thomas C Schelling, *Arms and Influence*, New Haven: Yale University Press, 2008, p. 38.

11 Carl von Clausewitz, *On War* (trans. JJ Graham), London: Routledge & Kegan Paul, 1949.

12 Schelling, 2008.

13 John Herz, *International Politics in the Atomic Age*, New York: Columbia University Press, 1959.

14 WG East & OHK Spate, *The Changing Map of Asia: A Political Geography*, London: Methuen, 1961, p. 157.

15 Raoul Castex, *Strategic Theories* (trans. Eugenia C Kiesling), Annapolis: Naval Institute Press, 1994.

16 Christopher Small & Joel E Cohen, 'Continental Physiography, climate and the global distribution of human population', *Current Anthropology*, Vol. 45, No. 2, April 2004, pp. 269–76; Michel Lichter, Athanasios T Vafeidis, Robert J Nicholls & Gunilla Kaiser, 'Exploring data-related uncertainties in analyses of land area and population in "Low Elevation Coastal Zone" (LECZ)', *Journal of Coastal Research*, Vol. 27, No. 4, July 2011, pp. 757–68.

17 Canfei He, 'Industrial agglomeration and economic performance in transitional China', in Yukon Huang & Alessandro Magnoli Bocchi (eds), *Reshaping Economic Geography in East Asia*, Washington: World Bank, 2009, pp. 259–60.

18 International Maritime Organization, International Shipping Facts and Figures, Maritime Knowledge Centre, March 2012, www.imo.org/KnowledgeCentre/ShipsAndShippingFactsAndFigures/TheRoleandImportanceofInternationalShipping/Documents/International%20Shipping%20-%20Facts%20and%20Figures.pdf.

19 Geoffrey Till, *Seapower: A Guide for the Twenty-First Century*, London: Frank Cass, 2004, p. 284

20 Till, 2004, p. 71.

21 Till, 2004, p. 127

22 Till, 2004, p. 4.

23 James R Holmes, Andrew C Winner & Toshi Yoshihara, *Indian Naval Strategy in the Twenty-First Century*, London: Routledge, 2009, p. 72.

24 Till, 2004, p. 154.

25 John Lewis Gaddis, 'Containment: Its past and future', *International Security*, Vol. 5, No. 4, Spring 1981, p. 80.

26 Siemon T Wezeman, 'The maritime dimension of arms transfers to South East Asia, 207-11', in *SIPRI Yearbook 2012: Armaments, Disarmament and International Security*, Oxford: Oxford University Press, 2012.

27 Till, 2004, p. 149.

28 Samuel P Huntington, 'National policy and the Transoceanic navy', *United States Naval Institute Proceedings*, Vol. 80, No. 5, May 1954.

29 James R Holmes & Toshi Yoshihara, *Red Star Over the Pacific: China's Rise and the Challenge to US Maritime Strategy*, Annapolis: Naval Institute Press, 2010.

30 Ronald O'Rourke, *China Naval Modernization: Implications for U.S. Navy Capabilities – Background and Issues for Congress*, Congressional Research Service, 23 December 2014.

31 Holmes, Winner & Yoshihara, 2009.

32 Desmond Ball & Richard Tanter, *The Tools of Owatatsumi: Japan's Ocean Surveillance and Coastal Defence Capabilities*, Canberra: ANU Press, 2015.

33 Sam Bateman, 'Perils of the deep: The dangers of submarine proliferation in the seas of East Asia', *Asian Security*, Vol. 7, No. 1, 2011, pp. 61–84.

34 Ronald E Ratcliff, 'Building partners' capacity: The thousand ship navy', *US Naval War College Review*, Autumn 2007.

35 Julian S Corbett, *Some Principles of Maritime Strategy*, Annapolis: Naval Institute Press, 1988 [1911], p. 91.

36 MJ Pintado, *Portuguese Documents on Malacca*, Kuala Lumpur: National Archives of Malaysia, 1993, pp. 245–6.

37 Holmes & Yoshihara, 2010.

38 For example, Jean-Paul Rodrigue, 'Straits, passages and chokepoints: A maritime strategy of petroleum distribution', *Cahiers de Geographie du Quebec*, Vol. 48, No. 135, December 2004, pp. 357–74; John Daly, 'Naval choke points and command of the sea', *World Politics Review*, 2 March 2009; Charles Emmerson & Paul Stevens, *Maritime Choke Points and the Global Energy System*, Chatham House Briefing Paper EERG 2012/01, January 2012.

39 CE Calwell, *Military Operations and Maritime Preponderance: Their Relations and Interdependence*, Edinburgh: William Blackwood & Sons, 1905, pp. 266–7.

40 Janet L Abu-Lughod, *Before European Hegemony: The World System AD 1250–1350*, New York: Oxford University Press, 1989.

41 Russell Hsiao, 'Sanya nuclear submarine base shakes Asian neighbours', *China Brief*, Vol. 8, No. 10, The Jamestown Foundation, 13 May 2008.

42 Leszek Buszynski & Christopher B Roberts (eds), T*he South China Sea Maritime Dispute: Political, Legal and Regional Perspectives*, Abingdon: Routledge, 2014.

43 Holmes, Winner & Yoshihara, 2009, p. 44.

44 David Brewster, 'The Bay of Bengal: A new locus for strategic competition in Asia', *Asia Pacific Bulletin*, No. 263, East–West Centre, 15 May 2014.

45 Lawrence G Potter & Gary G Sick (eds), *Security in the Persian Gulf: Origins, Obstacles, and the Search for Consensus*, New York: Palgrave, 2002.

46 Robert Hunter, *Building Security in the Persian Gulf*, Santa Monica: RAND, 2010.

47 Christopher M Davidson, *The Persian Gulf and Pacific Asia: From Indifference to Interdependence*, London: Hirst, 2010.

48 Calwell, 1905, p. 266.

49 Alan J Levine, *The Pacific War: Japan Versus the Allies*, Westport: Praeger, 1995.

50 Holmes & Yoshihara, 2010, p. 94.

51 Ashutosh Misra, *India and Pakistan: Coming to Terms*, London: Palgrave, 2010.

52 Marc Lanteigne, 'China's maritime security and the "Malacca Dilemma" ', *Asian Security*, Vol. 4, No. 2, 2008, pp. 143–61.

53 Allan Collins, *Security and Southeast Asia: Domestic, Regional and Global Issues*, Singapore: ISEAS, 2003.

54 Mark Mancall, *Russia and China: Their Diplomatic Relations to 1728*, Cambridge: Harvard University Press, 1971, pp. 20–5.

55 Richard Pipes, *Russia Under the Old Regime*, Harmondsworth: Penguin, 1974, p. 55.

56 Michael E Clarke, *Xinjiang and China's Rise in Central Asia: A History*, London: Routledge, 2011.

57 Peter B Golden, *Central Asia in World History*, New York: Oxford University Press, 2011.

58 Lena Jonson, *Vladimir Putin and Central Asia: The Shaping of Russian Foreign Policy*, London: IB Tauris, 2004.

59 David Christian, *A History of Russia, Central Asia and Mongolia*, Oxford: Blackwell, 1998.

60 Vladimir Paramonov, *Russia in Central Asia: Policy, Security and Economics*, London: Nova Science, 2009.

61 Bobo Lo, *Axis of Convenience: Moscow, Beijing and the New Geopolitics*, Washington: Brookings Institution Press, 2008.

62 Sally M Cummings, *Understanding Central Asia: Politics and Contested Transformations*, New York: Routledge, 2012.

63 Robert L Canfield & Gabriele Rasuly-Paleczek (eds), *Ethnicity, Authority and Power in Central Asia: New Games, Great and Small*, London: Routledge, 2011.

64 Clarke, 2011.

65 AV Malashenko, *The Fight for Influence: Russia in Central Asia*, Washington: Carnegie Endowment for International Peace, 2013.

Chapter 6 Asia and the World

1 Richard Dobbs, Jaana Remes, James Manyika, et al., *Urban world: cities and the rise of the consuming class*, McKinsey Global Institute, Washington, DC, 2012.

2 Michael Wesley, 'The new bipolarity', *The American Interest*, Vol. 8, No. 3, Winter 2013.

3 For example, in relation to China, see William A Callahan, *China: The Pessoptimist Nation*, Oxford: Oxford University Press, 2010.

4 For example, Kwai-Chung Lo, in Otmazgin & Ben-Ari, 2012.

5 An example of the Panglossian school is the Australian Government's 2012 White Paper, *Australia in the Asian Century*; of the Hobbesian school is Aaron L Friedberg's 'The geopolitics of strategic Asia, 2000–2020', in Ashley J Tellis, Andrew Marble & Travis Tanner (eds) *Strategic Asia 2010–2011: Asia's Rising Power and America's Continued Purpose*, Seattle: NBR, 2010.

6 Xu Shiquan, *Sunflower Movement and Cross-Strait Relations*, Stiftung Wissenschaft und Politik Discussion Paper, September 2014.

7 Richard A Bitzinger, 'China's double-digit defense growth', *Foreign Affairs*, 19 March 2015.

8 Robert Gilpin, *War and Change in World Politics*, Cambridge: Cambridge University Press, 1981.

9 Andrew Erickson & Gabe Collins, 'The long pole in the tent: China's military jet engines', *The Diplomat*, 9 December 2012.

10 Kwang Ho Chun, *The BRICs Superpower Challenge: Foreign and Security Policy Analysis*, Farnham: Ashgate, 2013.

11 For example, see Edwin M Truman, *IMF Reform is Waiting on the United States*, Peterson Institute for International Economics, Discussion Paper No. PB14-9, Washington, 19 March 2014.

12 Ryuzo Sato, Rama V Ramachandran & Myra Aronson (eds), *Trade and Investment in the 1990s: Experts Debate on Japan–US Issues*, New York: New York University Press, 1996.

13 See Michael Wesley (ed.), *Energy Security in Asia*, London: Routledge, 2007.

14 Simon Denyer, 'Chinese tighten their grip on internet', *Sydney Morning Herald*, 31 January 2015.

15 Eric Helleiner, *Forgotten Foundations of Bretton Woods: International Development and the Making of the Postwar Order*, Ithaca: Cornell University Press, 2014.

16 Mandy Zuo & Kwong Man-ki, 'Chinese leader Xi Jinping spells out ambitious Asia vision at Boao Forum', *South China Morning Post*, 28 March 2015.

17 Quoted in Paul Keal, *Unspoken Rules and Superpower Dominance*, London: Macmillan, 1983, p. 142.

INDEX